Why Aren't You Thriving?

ENDORSEMENTS

"Rousing. Insightful. Empowering. Sam's perspective in *Why Aren't You Thriving?* will challenge your mind and stir your soul to an even higher level of thriving!"

— **Dr. Jarrod Spencer**, sports psychologist and
author of *Mind of the Athlete:
Clearer Mind, Better Performance*

"At a time when being pro-guy is pretty uncommon or even unpopular, *Why Aren't You Thriving?* not only assumes that men should be thriving as God created, but gives us a roadmap to do just that. I challenge you to ask yourself this tough question and use the tools in Sam's book to build the exciting life God destined you to live!"

— **David Benham**, bestselling author and
nationally-acclaimed entrepreneur

"When I help people create online businesses, there's one thing that holds back more people than anything else: wondering if they can do it. I loved tackling this topic with Sam in the Mission chapter of *Why Aren't You Thriving?*. His approach to helping men show up in all areas of their lives is honest, accessible, and actionable. Get Sam's book and flip your life!"

— **Shane Sams**, CEO & Founder of
FlippedLifestyle.com

"The most common question I get from my success coaching clients is, 'Can I really do it all? Can I perform at a high level in my marriage, my career, and my health?' It's understandable to have doubts because most people aren't. BUT… there's good news. If you're equipped with the tools, stories, and strategies that Sam provides in this power-packed book, you'll be able to THRIVE in the most important areas in your life! I encourage you to dig in and discover how to start thriving today."

— **Mitch Matthews**, Success Coach and
Founder of the *Dream Think Do* Podcast

"As an elite men's coach, I help Christian husbands, dads & business owners 'blow up rocks' in their heads, targeting the lies and false beliefs that are holding them back from really living. The *Why Aren't You Thriving?* assessment is a great first step to identifying the rocks that are keeping you from thriving in your life. If you want to thrive, read Sam's book now."

— **Joseph Warren**, Elite Men's Coach at
BlowUpRocks.com and host of #1 podcast *Broken Catholic*

"Your life is the product of the questions you risk asking yourself. Sam asks a profoundly important question, then guides you step-by-step to the answers. If your life is good, but you're wondering if it could be great, move *Why Aren't You Thriving?* to the top of your stack."

— **Eric Nevins**, Founder of
Christian Podcasters Association

"As a Licensed Marriage and Family Therapist and High Performance Marriage Coach, I've seen it time and time again: Men have all the things they 'think' they should have, but they all feel like something is missing. Sam helps readers focus on what's missing and then gives guidelines and practical steps to fill the gaps that we all have felt. Grab *Why Aren't You Thriving?* and thank him later!"

— **T. Seth Studley** M.S., LMFT; Speaker, Author, Podcaster, and Coach at AnatomyOfUs.com

"Why Aren't You Thriving? is the challenge and encouragement that all men need. The questions in Sam's book are tough, meaningful, and can help provide a waypoint as we continue to become the men that God has designed us to be. Step out of your comfort zone a bit and allow yourself to be challenged to thrive. You won't regret it."

— **Dr. Bryan Hendley**, creator of *The Purpose Project*

"Just reading the introduction I was struck with a lightning bolt of truth: if you want a better life, you must ask better questions. *Why Aren't You Thriving?* has the questions to help eliminate all your pain and problems."

— **Evan Money**, Ph.D, happily married, #1 Bestselling Author & global entrepreneur

"Sam's book reminds us that God did not create us simply to survive, but to thrive, and we can only do that when we live integrated lives. As a husband, father, and psychologist, I used to see myself and my life as compartmentalized, fragmenting my identity and putting me in conflict with others. In *Why Aren't You Thriving?*, Sam does a great job of demonstrating how we can build our lives one success at a time until we're thriving in all core areas—and doing so with authenticity and integrity!"

— **Dr. Andy Garrett**, psychologist; founder of the True North Blueprint; world's leading authority| in the psychology of identity

"*Why Aren't You Thriving?* is a challenge to any man who is looking for more from life. But instead of the posturing and posing that many gurus offer today, Sam invites us to join him on a journey and gives us the tools we need along the way."

— **Ryan James Miller**, business consultant and performance coach, host of *Authentic Conversations*

"I'm passionate about helping dads write their Legacy Letter, something they can pass on to their children. *Why Aren't You Thriving?* is a call to dads—and men of all ages—to start living that legacy right now… and even provides many of the examples that most men are missing!"

— **Blake Brewer**, Founder of the Legacy Letter Challenge

"John Piper said, 'Books don't change people: paragraphs do. Sometimes even sentences.' *Why Aren't You Thriving?*, because of the authentic and vulnerable contributions of so many individuals, is FULL of paragraphs and sentences that can change your life. You'll want to keep it as a field guide to remind you HOW to thrive as you move through the seasons of life."

> — **Brian Robinson**, bestselling author and host of the *Real Faith Stories* podcast

"Sam has created a masterpiece with *Why Aren't You Thriving?*. Designed to help men reach their full potential at any point in time, he's done it and so much more. By targeting the desire every human has to become their best, and tying his vision to a practical approach, Sam helps men thrive. For anyone with a desire to thrive, this is a must-read!"

> — **Femi Doyle-Marshall**, Founder of RebootX Academy

"I love working with dads who want to do better and be better for their families, but many of them aren't sure whether they have what it takes. Fortunately, Sam set out to learn how to thrive in all seven areas of life and has provided many of the answers in *Why Aren't You Thriving?* You have what it takes. Read Sam's book to find out how to do it!"

> — **Cam Hall**, Founder of Fight the Dad Bod and the Dads Making a Difference mastermind

"In a world of 'good enough,' Sam offers us a roadmap for thriving. *Why Aren't You Thriving?* is just the beginning of the conversation; how it ends is up to you!"

— **Alex Demczak**, Co-author of
*The Sale: The Number One Strategy
to Build Trust and Create Success*

"What an insightful read that is much needed for men today! As a husband, father of five, and entrepreneur, *Why Aren't You Thriving?* spoke to me on many levels. Sam's book will help remove blind spots and equip you with the clarity to thrive like never before. Well done, Sam!"

— **Jose Escobar**, Founder & CEO of
The Entrepreneur's Bookshelf

WHY
AREN'T YOU
THRIVING?

A Man's Guide to Asking
Tough Questions and
Getting Better in 7 Core Areas

SAM FEENEY

NEW YORK

LONDON • NASHVILLE • MELBOURNE • VANCOUVER

Why Aren't You Thriving?

A Man's Guide to Asking Tough Questions and Getting Better in 7 Core Areas

Published in New York, New York, by Morgan James Publishing. Morgan James is a trademark of Morgan James, LLC. www.MorganJamesPublishing.com

Proudly distributed by Ingram Publisher Services.

Morgan James BOGO™

A **FREE** ebook edition is available for you or a friend with the purchase of this print book.

CLEARLY SIGN YOUR NAME ABOVE

Instructions to claim your free ebook edition:
1. Visit MorganJamesBOGO.com
2. Sign your name CLEARLY in the space above
3. Complete the form and submit a photo of this entire page
4. You or your friend can download the ebook to your preferred device

ISBN 9781631959417 paperback
ISBN 9781631959424 ebook
Library of Congress Control Number: 2022935990

Cover Design by:
Megan Dillon
megan@creativeninjadesigns.com

Interior Design by:
Christopher Kirk
www.GFSstudio.com

Morgan James is a proud partner of Habitat for Humanity Peninsula and Greater Williamsburg. Partners in building since 2006.

Get involved today! Visit MorganJamesPublishing.com/giving-back

DEDICATION

To Marita
Thanks for asking the question that began this journey
and for making the journey so worthwhile

TABLE OF CONTENTS

Acknowledgments xv
Foreword xix
Introduction: When Good Enough Isn't
                          Good Enough. 1
Preface: How to Use This Book 13

Chapter One: Identity 17
Chapter Two: Faith 33
Chapter Three: Mission 49
Chapter Four: Relationships 65
Chapter Five: Health 103
Chapter Six: Finances 121
Chapter Seven: Career 139
Chapter Eight: The Answer to the Question 157

Conclusion: What Do I Do Now? 165
About the Author 169

ACKNOWLEDGMENTS

'm so grateful for the opportunity to write this book, and—like everything else in my life—I couldn't have done it without a lot of help from a lot of people.

I thank God for the gift of vision and for the connections and timing He orchestrated to bring together all the amazing contributors to this book. Unless the Lord builds the house . . .

My wife Marita and my children—Cole, Cora, Cade, Clay, and Cowan—are integral parts of this book because they allowed me the time over the summer of 2021 to record all the podcast interviews when I could (should?) have been playing with them. Of course, they're the reason

I'm on this mission; lessons like the ones in this book are part of the legacy I'm trying to live for them.

Iron Sharpens Iron's mastermind groups, especially True North (Paul Edwards, Raul Figueroa, Scott Hooper, Steve Kinsley, Zach Lush, Jeff Ristine, Chad Stokes, Aaron Walker, Gary Wilburs, and Chuck Wood), provided me the perspective and the encouragement to develop the Made to Thrive brand and the framework for this book.

To the contributors of this book: I truly couldn't have done it without you. Thank you for giving your time as a guest on the podcast, for sharing openly and honestly about your journey to thriving in a specific area of your life, and for being an encouragement to all of us who want to do better and be better for those around us! They are:

Dean Allison, Allen Arnold, Omar Barlow, Brad Barrett, Scott Beebe, Lance Belline, Clark Bradley, Blake Brewer, Seth Buechley, Adam Carroll, Joel Cochran, Adam Connors, Kevin Davis, Luciano Del Monte, Femi Doyle-Marshall, Nate Dukes, Erik Dixon, Paul Edwards, Dr. Andy Garrett, Jim Gromer, Cam Hall, Russ Hedge, Bryan Hendley, Curtis Hunnicutt, Rich Lewis, David Littlejohn, Nick Matiash, Mitch Matthews, Ryan Miller, Evan Money, Jimmy Page, Warren Peterson, Stefan "Steph" Pettersson, Anil Ramdin, Brian Robinson, Shane Sams, Morgan Snyder, Seth Studley, Curtis Swisher, Jon Vroman, and Joseph Warren.

The Reluctant Thought Leader team really pulled this all together, gleaning the best content from my interviews into the meat of this book. Thanks to Eleni Aman, Cody Churchill, Paul Edwards, Kenah Fuller, Gideon Harris, and Devon LeMaster. Special thanks to Cody, who also edited the final manuscript; any grammatical decisions you have issue with probably are me overriding his advice.

Finally, thanks to everyone at Morgan James for helping me publish my first "real" book. It's so much fun to connect with you via a book, and I'm grateful to them for making it possible!

FOREWORD

I f I could undo the event in my life that started my journey to thriving today, I might have trouble saying "Yes," even though it would save a life.

At the end of July 2001, I was firing on all cylinders: a beautiful wife, two daughters, more than twenty years of success in business and no signs of slowing down. I had all the "stuff" that was supposed to make me happy—cars, homes, boats, money, friends, and vacations. But when the clock ticked into August of that year, everything changed—and nothing's been the same since.

On the first day of that month, I struck and killed a pedestrian while driving through my hometown of Nashville, Tennessee. I was not at fault; witnesses confirmed the pedestrian was disoriented and walked straight into my line of travel. But that didn't change the fact that I'd ended a human life. I had to learn to live with a new reality I couldn't undo, and it took me five years to adjust.

Early on in my marriage to Robin, my wife, I told her, "I don't want to be broke all my life." I had an entrepreneurial bug, and I'd grown up poor. At the tender age of nineteen, I thought making a ton of money would scratch the itch. And for a while, it did. Statistically, it makes a huge difference for the average adult, up to the first $70,000 of annual income.

But once you pass that threshold, it gets harder and harder for success to have the same effect. It's almost like you develop a "tolerance" for it, the way you would for a prescription painkiller. It didn't matter; I spent the first two decades of my career trying to make up for all my weaknesses by earning more and more money . . . Until the day I came home with a pocketful of money to a house full of strangers.

Sam's vision and mission for men has the same healthy appreciation for success that we've worked hard to create in the Iron Sharpens Iron mastermind. As a creator-developer personality, I don't think I could participate in a "money-less" existence, like living in a commune or surviving off-the-grid. If you read this book and think anything other than "Sam wants his readers to succeed and prosper," you're missing the point. The problem for many men is that success becomes their god. They get tunnel-vision focused on achievement and acquiring more, long after the whistle blows, and they need to make the shift from success to significance.

Sam's book is really about significance. That's what thriving is and what it does; it doesn't only help you and your immediate family. Your life begins to have a ripple effect that impacts your friends, colleagues, associates, community, church, and country—wherever you show up. This is what's lacking when men don't thrive, regardless of the size of their pocketbook or how many popularity contests they win. I know this journey well; I've been down it a few times. The last thing I wanted was for my life and legacy to read: "Poor kid from Nashville makes enough to retire at age twenty-seven. Nobody cares." I needed to do something more than make another million dollars. To get the true rewards of Sam's book, you have to start by pulling back the curtain. I lead mastermind groups today because a now-famous gentleman called Dave Ramsey invited me to join one. I was afraid, and didn't want to participate. Dave was (and is) such a hard-charging and intelligent guy, and I didn't want him to know about all my faults and failures. But I went anyway, and I was shocked to learn—Dave, Ken Abraham, Dan Miller and every other man in that group— also had problems! They, too, had struggles, failures, and issues with maturity that they felt uncomfortable sharing. I see now that their success was because they chose to share it rather than continue to hide.

I've long believed the quote from Jim Rohn: "You are the average of the five people you spend the most time with." What I learned from working with those men, I now pass to younger men like Sam. You have every reason to believe he pursues the same success and significance and wants to help men like you (or the men you love if you're a lady reading this) change your family tree for the better. I won't lie to you—Sam's objective isn't to get you to "like" him. It's to make you better. Often, that means telling the truth, and not everyone's in a place to hear the truth. But I can promise you this: Nobody becomes better by believing sweet-sounding lies. As Oliver Cromwell said, "He who stops being better, stops being good."

When you begin your journey into significance, you should begin to ask the right kind of questions more frequently. As this happened for me, I started to ask:

"How can I do things more efficiently?"

"How can I make this more profitable?"

"How can I serve my customers better?"

"How can I provide more value to people?"

"How can I meet more amazing people?"

"Who should I surround myself with to get where I want to go?"

"Who can help me improve in the areas where I'm the weakest?"

If you can find answers to those questions, I believe you'll thrive in ways you can't imagine. But there's always a risk you take: Things might not work out the way you think they will. In some cases, it can take years to undo bad habits, upper limit challenges or blind spots. If you find hope when you read Sam's discoveries, that's a good start. But you'll need to risk failure if you want to reach the promised land of thriving. To this, I can only say that if you're already not thriving, you've got everything to gain and nothing to lose by following Sam's advice.

I love how Sam's podcast, *Made To Thrive*, opens by saying "Let's thrive together." There's no such thing as excellence in isolation. In addition to what he shares in this book, I want to strongly recommend you find community in his mastertermind groups. I've read enough books to know that the gold Sam has for you will soon turn to "rust" in your mind without a board of trusted advisers gathered around you. Coaching and masterminds provide you with speed, knowledge, relationships, and accountability. The truth is that, by ourselves, we're all a bunch of knuckleheads, but together, we can solve problems, side-step landmines and encourage each other to grow, mature and thrive. This is the biggest advantage I have in life, marriage, and business—other strong men of faith sharpening me while I help sharpen them.

It's a privilege to ring the bell at the start of Sam's book, and I hope you find what you're looking for. Now, let's thrive together.

— *Aaron T. Walker*
Founder of Iron Sharpens Iron masterminds
and author of *View From the Top*

Introduction:

WHEN GOOD ENOUGH
ISN'T GOOD ENOUGH

Cohn: "I can't stand it to think my life is going so
fast and I'm not really living it."
Jake: "Nobody ever lives their life all the way up
except bull-fighters."
— **Ernest Hemingway,** *The Sun Also Rises*

"The glory of God is a man fully alive."
— **St. Irenaeus**

1

The title of this book is a question you're meant to sit with for a few minutes every once in a while. It's an invitation to continue the journey you may have started years ago. One that's worth the work.

You see, I believe men are supposed to thrive, to succeed, to kick butt in every single area of their lives. (Yes, women are supposed to thrive too, but frankly, *Why Aren't Women Thriving?* is a book for someone else to write.) But we aren't. And it's painfully obvious to our families, our communities, and our world. If you're honest with yourself, you'll find one or two areas you struggle with, too. Maybe it's the usual suspects of faith and physical health, or maybe you're still struggling to make sense of your career or a broader mission in life. Regardless, practically none of us are thriving in all areas of our lives.

We know more information than ever, "connect" with more people than ever, and have shockingly more resources than the giants who came before us, yet most of us are just going through the motions. Yes, we probably do pretty darn well in one or two areas of our lives, but if you only work out one muscle group, you'll soon find yourself out of balance (and looking kind of weird).

When I ask, "Why aren't you thriving?" I confront your status quo and mine. I'm challenging the vast majority of men—not saying "You need to do more!" or "You need to try harder!"—to experience a higher level of existence, one closer than you think and more rewarding than you can imagine.

When you begin to ask yourself, "Why aren't I thriving?" you begin tapping into the still, small voice you hear when your attention drifts in church, just before you fall asleep or on the drive home from watching an action movie. You start to look for an answer to the question, "Is this all there is?"

"Is this all there is?"

What does it mean to thrive? If I write a book asserting that men aren't thriving, it would make sense to figure out what thriving really means, right?

The genesis of *Made to Thrive*, which includes this book, the *Made to Thrive* podcast, and everything else at madetothrive.coach, began with an unassuming question my wife asked me a few years ago:

"Is this all there is?"

Her question wasn't a condemnation of our marriage or of the life that we had created together. Both of those were going pretty well, actually. We had three (now five!) beautiful children, we lived in a great neighborhood, I had a job that paid me well, and we felt happy with our church.

No, her question didn't express discontent with what was, but speculated about her expectations for the next fifty or sixty years. Though she asked me, she really pointed the question to God, the universe and to life itself. The question haunted me as well: *Is this the best I can expect? Is there something more that I'm missing out on?* Henry

David Thoreau put it well when explaining his two-year retreat to the woods of New Hampshire:

"I went to the woods because I wished to live deliberately, to front only the essential facts of life, and see if I could not learn what it had to teach, and not, when I came to die, discover that I had not lived. I did not wish to live what was not life, living is so dear . . ."

We decided we wanted to live deliberately, too. So, we started looking around for people who were thriving, who were living "all the way up" in every area of their lives, but we found it much more challenging than we expected. Was there some hidden formula for thriving we didn't have access to? Was anyone really "fully alive" and, if so, what did that look like?

My Journey to Good Enough

Identifying what you don't want sometimes serves as the simplest way to identify what you do want. So, if you want a picture of what thriving isn't, we can use my late teens and most of my twenties as an example.

Things started out well enough as I left high school and began college; I had career aspirations and a life design that included many of the good things, including family and a pursuit of some larger purpose. However, my world became radically self-centered over the next few years, and not in the "put your oxygen mask on yourself first" way that leaves more for those around you. Sadly, I became a black hole of self-indulgence, and the people closest to me suffered the most. My grandiose vision for my life became a means of getting whatever I could in the moment with no regard for long-term effects.

It took me the better part of a decade, but I eventually tired of a lifestyle that would never truly provide fulfillment. I took a long look at the decisions I made and the outcomes they produced. I met my wife, sensed she was my last shot at a healthy relationship, and saw a therapist for four months to work on issues of identity at the root of my pattern of relational sabotage.

After a rocky first few years of marriage (I still needed to undo most of the selfish tendencies that had become habits), my journey from 'big fat jerk' to 'pretty good' was complete with the birth of our first child. All apologies to my wife, but Cole's arrival in my life gave me the outward-focused perspective I desperately needed to start living on purpose *with* purpose.

Is good enough still good enough?

After a few years of living as a good dad, a good husband and a contributor to society, I began to realize that I mostly lived by the Hippocratic oath, the one that doctors take during medical school: "First, do no harm."

Frankly—especially given my past—this was a pretty big deal, right? In fact, looking around at other men both today and over the past few millennia, this seems like an accomplishment! Men seem particularly good at screwing up what they've been entrusted with, so any man who doesn't intentionally cause harm to those around him is way ahead of the rest of the pack. A trophy, please!

But "not doing harm" doesn't equate to "doing good," and it certainly doesn't equal 'thriving.' Even with an extremely low bar for "good," barely exceeding it doesn't make a thriving man.

A scene from *Courageous*, a movie about thriving as a father, challenged my concept of "good enough." The characters exchange memories of their fathers and assess how they're doing in this area of their lives. When one dad maintains that he's "good enough," another pushes back, asking if that's really what his son deserves.

I gradually began examining my life in the 7 Core Areas (more on that in a minute) to determine whether I found myself settling for good enough, and—as you might have guessed—what I saw disappointed me. I was not thriving, not living all the way up or being fully alive. The way I lived—to answer my wife's question—really said, "Yes, this is it. This is all there is to live, and the best it can ever be."

Immediately, I saw the rest of my "good enough" life before me. I saw, in stark truth, the decades of the mundane, decades of not really "making a dent in the universe," as Steve Jobs said. Worst of all, I saw decades of an uninspiring example to my children of what life can be.

Because if you're honest with yourself (and now is the time to be honest with yourself!) the legacy you leave your children and those closest to you—the permission they need to become the truest version of themselves—is lived out in your daily life. If you play small, you'll teach them to do just that. In contrast, if you chase a life fully lived to the glory of God, they'll have that roadmap to use.

I need to thrive in all areas of my life.

So, why wasn't I already?

TWELVE REASONS WE DON'T THRIVE

When I sat down to figure out why I didn't live "all the way up," as Hemingway put it, I came up with the following reasons. They came to me as a result of conversations, observations and the honest self-evaluation this question demands. I also saw these reasons in many other men.

Like any scientist or researcher, I didn't use these potential reasons to beat myself up or give myself an out for not thriving; I simply made observations and some guesses before I set out to ask people who might know the answers.

In the same way, I invite you to use these as an informal inventory for yourself. If you have a physical copy of the book, you can simply check them off. If you have a digital copy, or are curious about your results, you can visit ami-thriving.com to take the survey and gain access to all the resources mentioned in this book.

Why aren't you thriving?
- ❏ You think you already are
- ❏ You think you're doing "good enough"

- ❑ You don't know that it's possible
- ❑ You don't believe you can do it
- ❑ You don't know anyone who is
- ❑ It seems like too much work
- ❑ You're afraid to fail
- ❑ You've tried and failed
- ❑ You don't know where to start
- ❑ You don't know how to persist when things don't go well
- ❑ You don't really see why you should
- ❑ You don't understand that you need to

The search for thriving begins.

Thrive (v.)

: to grow vigorously : FLOURISH

: to gain in wealth or possessions : PROSPER

: to progress toward or realize a goal despite or because of circumstances

My first step involved identifying all the areas in my life—in everyone's lives—that truly matter. My wife and I brainstormed the various facets of our existence, including those that affected us and those that affected those we love, and boiled it down to 7 Core Areas: Identity, Mission, Faith, Health, Career, Finances, and Relationships.

We didn't know exactly what it looked like or how to thrive in each of these areas, but it gave us a place to start. By the way, we'll dive into what each of those areas means and how to know whether you're thriving in them in the next chapter.

Once I had the 7 Core Areas, I began looking around for what Dr. Andy Garrett calls "exemplars," people who we can hold as examples of each area and learn from them. These people aren't perfect, but they have reached a certain level of success and therefore provide a roadmap of sorts for getting there. Andy himself is a contributor in the Identity section; I can't wait for you to meet him!

I began looking around for these exemplars—seemingly perfect men (no comment here from any of the ladies reading this!) who truly embody the 7 Core Areas and live "all the way up." At first glance, I seemed to have a shortage of available subjects. Did any man exist who thrived in all areas of his life? Was I chasing a unicorn?

I soon realized two things:

1. I needed to start my search by defining each of these 7 Core Areas one at a time, not in combination.
2. My "good enough" set point had attracted and maintained a good enough level of success in the 7 Core Areas. If I wanted to examine thriving, I had to dig deeper into my current relationships, look outside of them, or both.

Temporarily casting aside the search for men who thrive in all areas of their lives, I took a step back and began to look for isolated instances of thriving in specific areas. This was so I could learn from as many people as possible. As Emerson said, "Every man I meet is my superior in some way, and in that I can learn from him." It turns out most of us thrive in one, two, or even three areas of our lives, which encouraged me. If most of us have figured out how to succeed in parts of our lives, maybe we could do the same in others.

I started reaching out to people I already knew to ask them about how they were thriving in the 7 Core Areas. For those who wanted to really dig into a particular topic, I posed these questions about each Core Area:

1. Why aren't more men thriving in this area? What's holding them back?
2. When weren't you thriving in this area? What changed? What keeps you thriving?
3. What does it look like to thrive in this Core Area?
4. What tools, resources, strategies do you recommend?
5. What encouragement do you have for men to thrive in this area?

The conversations revealed quite a bit: Not only am I surrounded by thoughtful, intentional men who really care about making the most of life, but I was standing on Russell Conwell's acres of diamonds and not realizing it! Frankly, I felt a little upset that I had settled for surface-level relationships, limiting others' impact on my life by my comfort level. More on this revelation in the relationships chapter.

As I mentioned, I wanted to reach outside my network, since one's network largely reflects one's own values and goals. Put another way, you endure your network and your network endures you—to a point. If I was the limiting factor on my network, I was limiting the answers I would get. And the answers were important enough to get uncomfortable!

I started the *Made to Thrive* podcast as a resource to encourage, equip and empower people, and this platform became the perfect place to pursue this question: Why aren't men thriving? I asked for recommendations for interviews, reached out to or was connected to guys I had never met before, coaches, authors and "extraordinary Joes," and asked those same five questions. The content of the interviews I conducted make up the majority of this book, and I couldn't be more excited about what I found—and how I changed—along the way. I invite you to join me on your own journey to thrive in the 7 Core Areas. It will change your life!

Putting It All Together

As I noted earlier, I was initially stymied in my attempt to find men who fully lived out the 7 areas. However, as I went along my journey, I discovered a proven system for sustainable growth, one that allows me to create meaningful, consistent improvements in all areas of my life without compromising any of the success I've already realized. I'll share more about that in the last chapter. For now, let's learn how to use this book; it's likely different from other books you've read!

Preface:

HOW TO USE THIS BOOK

A writer only begins a book. A reader finishes it.
— Samuel Johnson

Books are mirrors: you only see in them
what you already have inside you.
— Carlos Ruiz Zafón

Let's start with a risky statement: I don't want you to read this entire book.

Does that surprise you? I've read a few books in my day. About fifteen percent of the content I read has bullseye value, while the rest kind of wasted my time.

I designed this book to fit *your* life, needs, and goals to build a meaningful experience during your stay on Earth. Personally, I think you'll get a lot out of studying the entire thing—but not all at once. Focus first on the ones that may hold you back from a truly rich life. If you know what those are, great! But if you want to be sure, I've prepared a five-minute assessment at amithriving.com. You'll get immediate feedback on what areas require the most work, which will tell you which chapters you should read first. Everyone wins—especially you—if you start working on meaningful change in your life.

How to Read Each Chapter

Each chapter follows the same format:

1. What "good enough" looked like in a given Core Area until I decided to start thriving.
2. The big lessons provided by our expert contributors, using the 5 Big Questions.
3. The 5 Big Questions for your life, which you can answer immediately.
4. Resources to learn more about the Core Area, including free access to our interviews.

The 7 Core Areas

1. **Identity**: The deepest, truest, most permanent (and good) version of yourself. You can't suppress it, destroy it or lose it. It's who you are and who you're becoming.

2. **Faith**: How you think about God, connect with Him and what you do with your relationship to Him. The way your deepest beliefs "bleed over" into other areas of your life.

3. **Mission**: The unique purpose and calling you exist to fulfill. Your passions, interests, talents, and abilities used for the right reasons, at the right time/place, with the right people.

4. **Relationships**: The quality and quantity of your connections with God, spouse, children, extended family, friends, acquaintances, and business associates / colleagues. We've added specialized subsections on marriage, fatherhood, and brotherhood (community).

5. **Health**: Your attentiveness and self-discipline to maintain and improve your physical body. How you eat, sleep, exercise and treat your body year-round.

6. **Finances**: Your short-term and long-term relationship with money—budgeting, spending and saving. Investing, giving and creating generational wealth.

7. **Career**: Your daily means of serving your fellow human beings and earning a living. How you emphasize your value to employers or customers.

Find the areas that apply most directly to you, and let's get thriving!

Chapter One:

IDENTITY

What a man can be, he must be.
— **Abraham Maslow**

In the social jungle of human existence, there is no
feeling of being alive without a sense of identity.
— **Erik Erikson**

Western culture infamously puts the cart before the horse, telling men for centuries that their principal value and identity lie in what they do for a living. This drives us to polar ends of the spectrum. In a seemingly positive way, society rewards men who excel at something—sports and business—come to mind. It works wonderfully, until you get displaced by a better performer. But when a man is on top, he's untouchable—and often, unreachable. Who can argue with a winner?

The pendulum swings the other way, too. Men who abandon performance also receive a "protected" status—usually subsidized by taxpayers, and defended by media and culture. Do we challenge the poor man, or coddle him? Do we punish the criminal, or excuse his behavior? Should we insist the vagrant contribute to society, or should we throw money at him?

From this, men get the message: You're either crushing it, or you're a charity case. I've come across men who have tried to succeed and failed. It breaks my heart to hear the anger and resentment in their voices. I've also met plenty of men who have given up on most everything—and their apathy turns my stomach.

I first noticed this while counseling boys in school. By the age of fourteen, most boys effectively disqualify themselves for fifty percent or more of eligible occupations because of how parents, church, and society look at them. In a peer-approval environment like high school, boys make long-lasting, internal decisions about the world around them. The majority are driven by painful or negative feedback–criticism, ostracism, bullying or (in some cases) institutional disapproval.

In church, you might hear pastors tell men, "Stop counting yourself out of God's Kingdom," or "We need to get in the game when it comes to our family, work, and ministry." This sentiment attempts to tackle another reason men don't thrive: We simply don't believe we can. Maybe someone told you so directly, or you put two and two together by watching the lives of authority figures. If your dad was "good, not great," your teachers were slightly above-average, and you played on teams that won forty-to-fifty percent of their games, you might think life is, at best, a tie. Not a total loss. Definitely not a win.

The idea of playing not to lose describes modern masculinity in the West. Call it damage control, sin management or "medio-cracy." It's not thriving.

Why aren't men thriving in their identity? What's holding them back?

Men struggle with identity because they get external and internal validation confused. We don't grow up with good tools for measuring. It's like trying to gauge the depth of the ocean with a yardstick. Take grades, for example. As a career school counselor, I believe in report cards and skills assessment tests. They measure performance, but they can't define identity. How can a man know he's thriving internally if he doesn't have an identity he sees as real, true, and eternal? Can it truly be described by his achievements?

As I talked this through with the men in this chapter, I found several ways we chase identity from external sources. It may look different from one man to the next, but you can be sure we're all trying to avoid change on the inside where it really counts.

When weren't you thriving in identity?

I interviewed five men about identity on my podcast and asked them the big five questions. We started with a discussion of what their lives looked like before they understood and began thriving in identity.

Allen Arnold

After thirty years in publishing, Allen Arnold joined John Eldredge's team at Wild At Heart Ministries in Colorado Springs. He left a trail of wreckage in the wake. "My identity lay in what I accomplished," he told me, "So the more I did . . . the more I was. I based this on a fortune cookie motto I found one day at a Chinese restaurant. It said, 'The one who says "It can't be done" should get out of the way of the one already doing it.'" Allen certainly achieved a lot, but he wasn't thriving.

Once, prior to 9/11, Allen took a film crew on a small commercial flight to do a project for an author. Distracted by a phone call, he missed boarding the plane. The flight crew offered his seat to another passenger and began pushing away from the gate. Allen went up to the gate and argued with the attendant, demanding she stop the plane, so he could board. When she didn't cooperate, he went ahead and barged through, ran out onto the tarmac and stood in front of the plane. The bewildered pilots demanded to know, "What are you doing?!" Allen told them, "This is my plane. I'm getting on it. Kick the other guy off."

And would you believe it worked? The pilots removed the other passenger, Allen got aboard and went on with his day as planned. Apparently, that's how winning is done. At least, that's how it's done when you don't know who you are.

If you wonder why men aren't thriving, there's plenty of evidence our culture exalts winning over character. The wake-up call came one day when Allen's boss took him to lunch, looked him in the eyes and said, "You're the most productive and efficient leader we've ever had, and everyone on your team thinks you're a complete jerk." What would you have said if you'd been in Allen's shoes that day? How much would it sting to find out what the majority of people in your life really think of you?

Dr. Andy Garrett

Growing up in a fatherless home, Dr. Andy Garrett entered adolescence deeply insecure. He spent most of his waking moments seeking approval and identity from peers, as many teenage boys do. "I wrestled with a lot of anger, anxiety and depression," he said. "I went from one external source to the next, trying to find my identity. I didn't know how to make the transition from adolescence into the person I wanted to become."

On the positive side, Andy had someone who figured strongly in his life—his grandfather, Carl Karcher, founder of the Carl's Jr. / Hardee's fast food chain. Andy grew up with consistent exposure to a man rooted deeply in identity, faith, and mission. "He was my best friend for many years," Andy recalled. "He built a worldwide business, was very successful, had thousands of employees, yet his most valuable and greatest success was who he was as a person. He was a masterclass in authenticity and how to treat people. He had such clarity, certainty, and integrity. Despite running a huge company, he had twelve kids and made sure he was home for dinner every night."

Years later, when challenged by a coach to think of what he truly wanted out of life, Andy thought of his grandfather. He coined the term "authentic exemplar" to describe Carl.

Why do so few men tap into the same kind of quality, depth, and strength Andy saw in Carl? As a clinical psychologist and life coach, he searches for the root causes behind personal and professional dysfunction. "Identity is something that applies to everyone, but all we're interested in doing is polishing the outside of an apple instead of nourishing the root," he told me. "We're trying to brush up the exterior. We learn about things that flow out of identity, but not the foundation where it starts."

Ryan Miller

Is it possible to avoid Allen's mistakes and be a "nice guy," as well as a productive and constructive citizen (to avoid Andy's mistakes), and still be empty on the inside? Ryan Miller—founder of the *Be Authentic* coaching program—said, "Yes."

A consummate son of southern California (tattoos and all), Ryan had the picture-perfect everything: A beautiful wife, two daughters, a gravy train career in sales and training salespeople and a pastoral role in a church. As with Allen, Ryan's life seemed to work wonderfully. He's good at selling (which usually simplifies the career area). He's athletic and loves CrossFit training. But a deep sense of emptiness lurked in the shadows. Ryan's exterior façade reached the end of its shelf-life in his mid-thirties.

"Highly driven, motivated people think, 'I've succeeded doing X, Y, and Z,'" Ryan said. "So, they keep doing X, Y and Z, thinking they'll be successful. The problem is, you reach a point where you feel like something's missing, but you don't know what it is. You feel like you have to keep achieving, but you also feel unfulfilled, like you lived somebody else's life. You're afraid to find out who you are. You settle for the façade you put out because you're scared to lose the success you've created."

At the peak of his sales coaching business, Ryan suddenly found himself under the gunfire of a madman in Las Vegas, at the Route 91 concert shooting in 2017. Ryan and his wife Michelle narrowly escaped the massacre. Several nearby attendees—including some of Ryan's friends—weren't so fortunate. In the aftermath, Ryan could not go back to "business as usual." He began a long season of digging deep, questioning everything, and evolving into an entirely new version of himself.

Joel Cochran

Joel Cochran, founder of Proclivity Fitness, emphasized how the victim mentality keeps us from thriving. He grew up in dire circumstances, the son of an absentee father and an emotionally volatile mother. "Victimhood is an acquired personality trait," he said. "If you walk around saying 'He did this,' 'She said that' or 'They don't like me,' you're already swimming in it. You allow the victim mentality into your soul, mainly by thinking destructive thoughts on a repetitive loop."

Joel made an inspired decision to pursue growth early in life, but as he grew into adulthood, he found himself crippled by self-sabotage. "I had to unlearn saying things like, 'I can't believe my dad made me feel that way!' Once I began to say, 'I can't believe I made myself feel that way,' it put so many more things back in my control. I learned to say, 'I can believe I made myself feel that way . . . and I'm going to change what I think.'"

Some men look at the duties and responsibilities they take on in life and "find validation in suffering and martyrdom," Joel explained. "They say things like 'I have to' or 'I'm forced to.'" In a terrible irony, he added, they also think themselves unworthy of compliments or affirmation.

Erik Dixon

Growing up as a Navy brat, Erik Dixon witnessed some terrifying moments that taught him, "The world is dangerous." Protesters stormed the gates of a Naval base in Japan where he lived with his family, and the only thing that stood between him and this angry mob was a group of U.S. Marines. "I could only see two possible outcomes," Erik said. "Either the Marines would open fire and kill the protesters, or they'd break down the gates and kill us. I determined from that moment on, I had to be hyper-vigilant, and I stayed that way until my mid-thirties."

Confusing your false identity with your real one makes it difficult to thrive with identity. He continued by saying, "Most of what men are told during their formative years comes from parents, and you have to come to terms with the fact that you are not any of those things." In other words, if your dad's words equated your identity with your behavior, then it's likely you have a false identity. Did he call you an idiot, a loser, or a failure? Did he hurl verbal abuse at you or express contempt for your natural personality and interests?

Don't think yourself exempt if your dad was a "snowplow parent" who refused to utter one critical word, either. It's false, any way you slice it. If your parents succumbed to the cultural pressure to never express criticism or disagreement, they also helped you create a false identity. "You're also not who you've 'decided' that you are," Erik added. "We call these ideas 'compensations.' The pressure we feel—because we don't measure up—to be strong, or fast, or first place. These become limiting beliefs, and we lock ourselves into them."

Ouch. Have you ever thought that way about yourself? I can feel the sting already from the times when I pre-defined myself based on my performance, and then publicly failed to live up to it. As masters of our own illusions, we hold ourselves back by recycling old narratives, from what we're told, or what we choose and infer from life around us.

How can you go from failure to thriving in identity?

Allen said the shift in identity came when he stopped trying to find it in temporary sources (other people or achievements) and looked for it in permanent ones (God).

"When you start to see things through God's lens, you can finally accept that His opinion is the only one that truly matters," Allen said. "I've learned to ask God, every morning before I get out of bed, 'What do You have for me today?' This sets a tone of expectancy instead of expectation. I also learned to end the day by laying down my interpretation and asking instead for His."

Andy told a fascinating, vulnerable story about a potential argument he diffused between himself and his wife. This proved to be a pivotal moment in his life. "She said something that stung," he admitted. "What she said was right, but I'm sensitive. My old way of dealing with this would be to 'get back at her,' by giving her the silent treatment. Instead, after thirty seconds or so, I realized: 'This isn't the husband I want to be. It's not how I want to show up, and it's not the evening I want to have.' So I made a joke out of it, and we ended up having a great night together."

The life-altering principle these men discovered comes from Dr. Abraham Maslow's hierarchy of needs. There are two kinds of self-esteem: external approval we receive from parents, peers, educators, employers, associates, and society; and internal approval that we receive into our innermost being. This is where we should co-author that identity with God.

We have to learn how to rank these two. Internal identity must come first, because for the overwhelming majority of men who aren't thriving, it's almost always neglected or ignored while we pursue external approval. You can't do this based on a carefully crafted public image, flying below the radar or making yourself a victim.

Erik realized one day that a lack of encouragement from his father didn't come from carelessness or negligence. As a teenager, he wrecked his car—famously, it turned out, by driving it through the backyard of the late Pat Bowlen, then-owner of the Denver Broncos football franchise. In a gesture Erik interpreted as a punishment and a curse, his father gave up Saturdays to take him to junkyards and find the parts and materials he needed to rebuild the car.

"My dad's love language was 'acts of service,'" Erik said, "while I just needed a lot of encouragement and 'words of affirmation.' So I took his response as punishment, and it wasn't until several years later that I could actually see how he was loving me. Once it became clear, I understood—not only had he loved me in a million different ways that I'd missed, but I'd also taken my attitude about him and projected it onto God."

Without the bias against God, Erik began to press deeper into true identity—his own and that of God. "In my freshman year of high school, they created a 'peer counseling' program and selected me to be one of the counselors," Erik recalled.

"I had no idea why at the time. I would sit and listen for hours to fellow students talk about abuse, violence in the home, food shortages, struggles with friends and breakups. Our constant objective was to meet people where they were in their current story and help them move into a new one. In hindsight, I can see how it set the stage for me to move into a better story of my own."

So, what about you? Could your current frustration, despair, anger, or other destructive emotions really be clues that you're being called forward? Is it possible, in a world full of illusions, that there's more to your story than you've accepted?

What does it look like to thrive in your identity?

Ryan and Michelle recently celebrated twenty years of marriage, after nearly crashing on the rocks of divorce in their fifth year. "We went on a crazy family trip this year when we had a conversation about how neither of us have ever experienced more joy," Ryan shared. "We're both very happy because we're helping each other be ourselves. The best part was hearing her affirm that in me, and that she felt it for herself too."

Allen experiments with trusting God in the unknown. He developed a node on his vocal cords from speaking at too many conferences and opted out of a surgical procedure to repair it. "I asked God about the surgery. I said, 'Is this what You have for me?' And He replied, 'Allen, it's your choice. You can choose to go to the doc, get it fixed, and everything will return to normal. Or you can cancel the surgery and enter into the unknown with Me. It's up to you.'"

Would you choose to cancel the surgery?

When Joel finally gave in and did the deep work on identity, his life improved dramatically. "My business skyrocketed over the last three-to-four months," he said. "'Thriving' means speaking with authority, loving yourself and recognizing the blessings you have. You shift from belittling yourself when you make mistakes to making light of it. I believe there are no true 'failures'; only success and blessings."

With his false self dismantled, Erik put his assumptions and conclusions on trial, one by one. He moved from the defense side of the courtroom to becoming the prosecutor.

"Take every limiting belief you have and ask, 'Is that actually true?' If you really get into it, you uncover the details. 'Is it true all the time?' 'Sometimes?' The deeper you get, the more you figure out you're more than 'good enough.' You're more than capable and worthy of love, but we take these little, tiny flaws and elevate them over the evidence."

Could you do this? Could you take the labels you've accepted on yourself, attach them to behaviors or incidents, and separate yourself from them? Could you observe what happened objectively, stripping it of all the meaning you used to attach so that you can actually do something about it? Keep identity in mind as you read the other chapters and sections of this book. It has a way of "spilling over" into the other categories. It's not just a "one-and-done" exercise you can forget about once you finish it. Identity will take your whole life to truly understand.

Is thriving in identity worth it?

You have the opportunity to live out of how God created you. He gave you authority to be the best you can be. You have to let yourself become that man. Maybe no one ever told you that you're a champion, but God certainly did. To look at yourself any other way will do you (and everyone you love) a disservice.

God seldom uses people with worldly "credentials." In fact, He has the habit of calling people into circumstances and situations where they feel underqualified. He does this so that it becomes impossible to maintain your false identity. In these situations, you begin to learn your true one. Carry a journal and writing utensil everywhere you go and write down what you hear. God isn't known for alerting us before He calls; He simply calls and waits for us to respond.

The world depends on men standing up to be who they were created to be. We have no chance of repairing the damage we've done by completely bulldozing masculinity. We're called to protect and provide for the people who need us the most. And the traditional, shallow definition of "provide" needs to change, because the greatest abundance we can provide in any scenario is ourselves.

And do the work! You can't automate this task with the push of a button or outsource it to someone else. Join the two percent of the world's population that takes action on this. That's what the world really requires from you—a man truly alive, bringing passion, purpose, and meaning in a place that seems more meaningless every day.

Let's not waste another second operating as our false selves. Let's go do the amazing and powerful things that happen when we truly come to life in our own skin.

Reminder: This book was designed to help you in the areas you need it most. If you're reading straight through, great! Keep going. If you're reading this chapter because you took the assessment and now want to jump to the last chapter instead of tackling other Core Areas, go ahead!

You can find additional resources for identity by listening to the Made to Thrive *podcast episodes featuring these men, or by visiting amithriving.com*

Chapter Two:

FAITH

Faith is taking the first step,
even when you don't see the whole staircase.
— **Dr. Martin Luther King, Jr.**

Faith does not eliminate questions,
but faith knows where to take them.
— **Elisabeth Eliot**

We have plenty of social institutions that say, "This is what faith looks like." You have your churches, mosques, synagogues, temples, religious organizations and associations. Rituals, observances, festivals, holidays and solemn occasions dot our calendar. Some of us even make time for faith through missions, businesses, ministries, projects, and causes.

But what about faith itself? What does the term mean in an age with so many expressions? Is it the presence or absence of religion? Is it tax-exempt or for-profit? Does it mean ceremonies and church attendance, or acts of charity and good works? Is it beliefs or behaviors?

In this chapter, we interviewed a group of unusual suspects, people for whom faith contains a degree of uncertainty. It's not a good idea to equate faith with certainty because . . . well, it isn't faith if you're certain, is it? To borrow a line from Inigo Montoya in *The Princess Bride*, I don't think "faith" means what we think it means. It's useful, in these situations, to start with the definition of the word in the dictionary:

1. Complete trust or confidence in someone or something.
2. Strong belief in God or in the doctrines of a religion, based on spiritual apprehension rather than proof.

Faith is how you think about God. What is He like? Can He be trusted? What does He want with you? It's also what you do to connect with God and what you make of your relationship with Him—much as you would with your wife and kids.

Faith is a process of consent and assent—allowing God to be who He is and not demanding explanations for everything. It's "knowing the unknowable God."

And as you'll see in this chapter, faith is different from success.

Why aren't men thriving in faith? What's holding them back?

Some people pine for the "good old days" when everyone went to church on Sunday and bowed their heads in prayer for the national anthem. Back then, society accepted and respected religion. Nowadays, depending on whom you talk to, it's a liability. Some men believe simply "showing up at church" equals thriving. They don't see why they should go any further; it represents a risk to their social standing or worldly occupation.

Another reason men fail to thrive comes from the belief that only mystics, monks, and ministers really need faith. It's an awful lot of work to truly believe hard enough so that God responds to your prayers. Did He answer the last time you prayed? Faith seems like a luxury for people with a lot of money, some special knowledge and the right connections, but not you.

Few men know anyone thriving in faith. In church, it somehow gets misinterpreted (or defined, in worse cases) by one's level of involvement. It centers on your degree of commitment and service as a ministry volunteer. That isn't helpful if twenty percent of the people do eighty percent of the work. That means four out of five believers don't thrive.

When weren't you thriving in faith?

As the son of a pastor, I had my own view of faith. I had no idea what to expect when I talked to men who thrived in this area due to my own preconceived notions. However, these conversations helped me develop a more mature, nuanced perspective of faith.

Rich Lewis

When Rich joined *Made To Thrive*, it struck me how relaxed and unhurried he seemed. Despite having plenty to say during the interview, I got the sense that he relentlessly pursues a strong faith in a relaxed manner. "I practice an Eastern religion in a Western culture," he said. "A lot of what I do can be traced directly back to Jesus. But the Western church is committed to the idea that 'faith' means 'following rules and codes of conduct.'

"The West simply doesn't have a lot of room for traditional Eastern practices like centering prayer, silence and listening for God to speak. That's a pity because many people are attracted to the idea of God speaking to them . . . but silence is a hard thing to do."

The pressure people feel to "have it all together," to keep up the appearance they're obeying all the rules is a classic misgiving about faith. It doesn't sound like a relationship that requires faith. Why would you need God if it's up to you to show Him how well you follow the rules? That's more like fulfilling an impossible contract, reinforced by guilt and shame.

Rich discovered that God takes an opposite approach from the religious establishment. "We don't realize God wants to help us process thoughts and emotions," he said. "Thomas Keating called it 'divine therapy.' We hold far too much tension and disconnect within ourselves. When we don't give them over to God, there's no space for Him to speak through the silence."

Morgan Snyder

Morgan believes men primarily settle for "small stories" in their lives. Working alongside John Eldredge and his team at Wild At Heart Ministries, he spent the last two decades observing the same pattern repeat itself. There are plenty of "stories" a man's life could fit; how can we tell which ones are real?

The way the modern church handles this reality doesn't impress Morgan: "Most men receive a 'benign' gospel— it's not worth living, and it ain't that great," he said. "So, if the story of God is small, our souls gravitate to the biggest stories we can find. To find our way to 'THE Story,' a man has to come to the end of himself. It has to get worse, before it gets better."

The occasion of his graduation from college was the first time Morgan looked in the mirror and saw, as he put it, "a soulless man. I had won the world—a 4.2 GPA, Barbie Doll girlfriend, class president for five years—but I'd lost my soul. If I'd died that night and had to face God . . . I'd have had nothing to say because my life was all posing."

Hearing Morgan's story was, honestly, a little relieving. I would describe my own college years as, "time well wasted." But if the star athlete, the valedictorian, magna cum laude stud with the bombshell on his arm ALSO feels like an empty shell?! Maybe I wasn't as bad as I gave myself grief for being all those years.

Mitch Matthews

Adding uncertainty to faith doesn't mean we have anything to fear. Fear is one of Mitch Matthews' blind spots. Who doesn't fear the unknown?

Mitch followed God along a very uncertain path as the chief source of energy behind the Big Dream Gathering. "I'm not a natural dreamer," he said. "In fact, if you check out my default settings, I'm more of a worrier than a dreamer. I'm more likely to imagine everything that could go wrong."

But on the verge of a dream's collapse in 2006, Mitch invited a group of people over to his home to share their dreams on paper and attach them to the walls. An event that was supposed to last one evening ended up taking a full week as the culture of encouragement and connections caught fire. "It was a classic example of something I've learned following God," he said. "Generally, you don't find the mission and then go; you go first, and then you find the mission."

"God nudged me in the direction of helping others pursue their dreams, so I could pursue my own," he added. "We invited thirty people to that first Big Dream Gathering, and twenty-nine of them showed up. When we asked them why they came, most of them said they'd forgotten or given up on their own dreams." In another forehead-slapping moment, Mitch realized that we cannot claim to love God if we don't love each other. It's difficult to ask for help if we don't live in community, and even harder to live in community if we're not helpful to others.

Brian Robinson

Here's another "curveball" story of faith. Brian Robinson's intimacy with God led him to create *Real Faith Stories*, a podcast that profiles Christian business owners who take enormous risks. But the idea came after months of a holding pattern, where Brian had no idea of what to talk about or who he wanted to target for his audience. Has that ever happened to you? Have you felt like God wants you to do something, yet He provides no details or specifics even if you ask Him?

Brian walked into several unknowns with no guarantee God would meet him there. "We sometimes say things like, 'If God shows up,'" he said. "But I think it's more accurate to say that if *we* show up with a step of faith, then God makes Himself real and gives us what we need."

Brian has recorded over sixty episodes of his show at the time of writing. But this journey started by walking away from the religious fog and pursuing a career in the (mostly secular) free market. He left a Lutheran / Presbyterian upbringing in Chicago, where there was a sense of faith but not much interest in Scripture.

Haunted by the idea that there was "more," Brian discovered the gifts of the Holy Spirit in college. He slowly detached from his traditional background and became an evangelical believer. His career, meanwhile, led into working for Fortune 500 companies like Johnson & Johnson, where he became a successful sales representative.

Then the road took a turn. Brian received an invitation from a friend to help start a business. Following a vivid, confirming dream from God, he accepted. And life took a turn for the worse—Brian went from company cars and name recognition in the business community to struggling to make a single sale. He had never been in a situation where he wouldn't eat if he didn't sell. Now he was parked on the side of a highway in Kansas, weeping and crying out to God to give him a sale.

"Something dramatic has to happen for us to turn to Jesus," Brian said. "I'd felt self-sufficient in my previous job. Now, I felt weak because I couldn't figure something out on my own. I realized this was God's way of humbling me and stripping me of pride. The brokenness I felt was actually His kindness, showing me how much I needed Him."

Does this give you an idea of what faith requires? If only it was as simple as saying, "I believe!" I saw and heard myself in this story. And I understood better why Brian wanted to collect similar stories on a podcast.

Joseph Warren

Joseph Warren's life, prior to meeting God, sounds like one many men would covet—at least on the surface. He enjoyed success leading a team of commercial real estate agents, and in his spare time he juggled relationships with five different girlfriends.

Gold, glory and girls—the three pitfalls that stalk any man of God. Why do these things keep working so well? Like fish in a sea, we keep getting hooked and don't learn from the traps others fall into. Joseph looked great on the outside—but inside, he was empty, bored, and miserable. "There was a bottomless pit of hurt I needed to fill, and I filled it with sexual relationships with girls," Joseph said. "It was like a drug, and I needed a fix."

Joseph's addiction brought him to a place of powerlessness and weakness. He couldn't stop himself and called out to God. "I said, 'I don't want to stop, so if You want me to stop, You gotta put the desire in my heart. I give You the permission to put the desire in my heart to give up my sexual addiction.'"

How can you go from failure to thriving with faith?

Let's revisit the definition of "faith" for a moment. It relies on certainty of the inherent goodness and reliability of something or someone. This stands in contrast to certainty in your own knowledge and understanding—the trap most men fall into. Pride is back again. We have pride in appearing to have things under control or our monopoly on doctrinal correctness. We feel proud of our ability to see the future or anticipate what God is up to. Not only that, but we take pride in our expectations and assume God will bless them just because we've been carefully following all the rules.

Rich's life changed dramatically when he learned to let God be God. "You drop your preconceived notions of who God is, how He shows up, what He does and how He does it," he said. This is a benchmark of humility in approaching and relating to God. Maybe we've missed it because we think spiritual humility only serves mystics, monks, and ministers. Rich isn't any of those things, but did he let his lack of qualifications stop him from growing in humility before God? Why should it be any different for us?

I can relate to God's perspective on pride. Have you ever been in a leadership role, only to discover the people you lead have their own ideas about how you should behave or what you should do? Have you ever been in authority over people and heard some of the ideas they vent about you when they don't think you're listening? If history can teach us anything, God's had no less trouble. If I were Him, I'd be glad to find just one person willing to let me be who I really am and not question it.

Morgan's journey to validation led him to understand the deep waters of his own heart and the ways his own motives had betrayed him. "Faith is always about the motives of the heart," he explained. "If I try to exercise that muscle without validation, it's rough. But if I've recovered my true heart and received validation from God, I get well and act from self-approval."

Mitch learned that God is, in fact, a dreamer. A big dreamer whose biggest obstacles in making dreams come true are the people He dreams for. "The missions of our lives get unveiled as we walk toward the essence of them," said Mitch, referring to the journey of maturity through surrender. Frequently, this takes the form of service to others first because God's essence is love, and love cares deeply about others. No wonder Mitch had to help others pursue dreams before he could fulfill his own.

Brian discovered God's generosity when he learned to sit quietly with his hands open. He offered a real-time example from the day before our interview. In 2018, he'd published a book, *The Selling Formula*, that became a #1 bestseller on Amazon. The day before we talked, he sensed a leading from God to offer a few chapters of the book for free on LinkedIn with a short video to announce it. After twenty unsuccessful attempts to shoot a quality video, Brian became frustrated. He felt unaccomplished, and before he could look around, the irritation had spiraled into feeling insecure about his entire future and value as a human being.

Time out! Has that ever happened to you? Have you ever flubbed something simple, and the next thing you know, your brain thinks that you might have to call it quits for good?

I'm glad I'm not the only one.

Joseph's Christian friends leveraged his interest in the opposite sex to lure him to a Wednesday gathering of believers. "They told me, 'There will be 100 pretty single girls there,' and I said, 'I'm in.' But when I got there, they brought up a billionaire speaker who gave testimony about surrendering his entire life and business to God. I'd never heard anything like that before."

Joseph fell in love with seeking God at a time when everything seemed to be going right. Yes, believe it or not, you don't have to be imprisoned or dying in a fox-hole to become a man of faith. You can also be called from a life that's going along swimmingly, at least by worldly standards.

What does it look like to thrive in faith?

"I have a bigger excitement for life, increased self-confidence and willingness to get out of my comfort zone," Rich said. "There's a deep peace and calm within me. I'm less prone to arguing and reacting to things. I'm quicker to listen and slower to speak. I'm excited about a future I can't see but not worried; I trust God implicitly."

There's a difference between communicated knowledge, which we get from parents, teachers, and the world; and revealed knowledge from God. "None of this came to me by going on the internet and using Google," Rich added. "You find it by going within. Once it takes root, you can then carry it forward into the world. But it's deep within us that God wants to show up."

Morgan learned a few phrases that gave him a voice to flex his faith. "Always be prepared to ask God if He is who He says He is" he advised. "Be ready and willing to surrender unconditionally: 'I give up everything to receive all You want to give me.'" Morgan also studied several older men through interviews and discipleship. "Go find older men and ask questions," he continued. "Ask them about what they gave up to become a man. Questions are the greatest access point to the soul."

When Morgan finally learned to ask, he found himself making a different request from God than most men would think to make: "Wreck the things I've built and show me what You want to replace them with."

Mitch discovered a deeper layer of being in the "sweet spot" with God. The Big Dream Gathering grew into a national movement, and today it's spreading even further via the "Dream Together" app, which brings the original event to worldwide digital availability. Strengthening relationships helped Mitch dream big, both for others and himself.

If God is kind, generous, and encouraging to you, why would He want anything different for His other children? Mitch learned to be ambitious for everyone, which ensured he got carried along for the ride. "That's the 'sweet spot' of living out faith," he said. "What some call 'flow,' I think of as the ability to do 'more of what God calls us to do, more often.' And while we're doing it, we also get to talk to Him about it as much as possible."

Joseph became enamored with spending quiet time in God's presence, seeking His counsel in full surrender. "God is such a gentleman that He waits to give Him permission by our own free will," he said. "To surrender and give up the whole mess and rely on His strength because ours is not enough. Everything changed when I did—God brought me my beautiful wife, I had a couple of kids, and I now help other men with similar problems."

When you thrive in faith, according to Joseph, the first thing to change is your sense of responsibility. "Men blame others, subconsciously, for not living the life they want," he said. "So I teach them: own your mess, surrender control, and give God permission to help you find your way out."

In his ninety-day coaching program, "Blow Up Rocks," Joseph's clients learn specific prayers that provide them with verbal "tools" to untangle themselves from a faithless mindset and existence. He takes them through the fire of surrender, the crucifixion of the ego and an awakening to the hope and joy of a life with family and love.

Their stories helped me. Have you ever tried to surrender your problems only to find they come back? If you're going to forgive people, simply saying "I forgive you" might not be enough unless you really mean it. I'm grateful for people who go the extra mile with faith.

Is thriving in faith worth it?

Maybe you've read this and thought, "Great. I have to get super spiritual, or even kind of weird, to be close to God." That's exactly the wrong idea. The journey toward intimacy with God takes time—and some of it will be quiet and seem fruitless. But that doesn't mean we shouldn't take it or that it's only for paid religious professionals.

In your early days, you can start with as little as sixty seconds. Take a minute to pause and ask God, "Will You come and speak to me?" It doesn't matter how busy you currently are. Everyone can find sixty seconds.

In fact, if God seems like a far-off reality only for the chosen few, the lives of the men who contributed to this chapter paint a different picture. The deep connection and sense of trust in God are not to be found only in huge historical moments, like the Exodus or the Resurrection, but rather in the daily activities and requirements of life. God resides in trips to the grocery store, interactions with your family, and the duties of your career.

The people we dismiss as having a "special" relationship with God are simply ahead of us when it comes to seeing this picture clearly. If you're powerful enough to create severe dysfunction in your life, you also possess the power to create order and happiness, with God's help.

But if you don't feel like you have enough belief in your tank—God's help hasn't changed. He has surrounded you with others to "hold faith," if you'll ask for help, so you can do the work. There is still a beautiful world outside the tunnel, even if you can't see the light at the end of it.

God wants to give you back a heart to believe. He wants you to have faith—to see what He sees—in His vision for your life. To do it this way, you have to consent to a slow, steady process of recovering authentic faith, taught personally by Him, in a way unique to you.

Faith looks different for each person when you get down in the weeds and examine it closely. If you learn to thrive in a properly aligned relationship with God and yourself, your unique brand of faith will "bleed" into the other 7 Core Areas.

In the next chapter, we'll take a closer look at Mission, and you'll see how thriving there frequently points back to Faith.

Reminder: This book was designed to help you in the areas you need it most. If you're reading straight through, great! Keep going. If you're reading this chapter because you took the assessment and now want to jump to the last chapter instead of tackling other Core Areas, go ahead!

You can find additional resources for faith by listening to the Made to Thrive *podcast episodes featuring these men, or by visiting amithriving.com*

Chapter Three:

MISSION

Every person above the ordinary has
a certain mission they're called to fulfill.
— **Johann Wolfgang von Goethe**

Everyone has his own specific vocation or mission in
life; everyone must carry out a concrete assignment that
demands fulfillment. Therein he cannot be replaced, nor
can his life be repeated. Thus, everyone's task is unique
as is his specific opportunity to implement it.
— **Dr. Viktor Frankl**

Our cultural idea of "Mission" has something in common with faith: We don't have many helpful preconceptions. If you picture orphanages in Africa, building houses in Latin America or teaching English to kids in Bangladesh, you have an incomplete picture of mission. Those are functions of mission. They are not the mission itself.

Mission begins much closer to home. You don't start by going statewide or national, or even citywide. It doesn't start in your front yard, backyard, or even inside your home. Your mission begins in you. It stems from a core set of beliefs cultivated through experience. Only then does it get reflected by the impact you make and the lifestyle you want to live. Mission is how you transform others on a deeper level.

Thriving in your mission means you operate at an abnormal level. You don't simply go through the motions. Instead, you become the kind of person whose impact radiates—who would, if called, lead a mission to Africa, Latin America or Bangladesh—and cause others to follow.

Your mission may include "success," but don't get it mixed up: Success isn't the point. Plenty of charitable organizations, churches, businesses, and non-government organizations have success figures. You can admire, touch, notice and connect them to the efforts of a person or group. But they won't provide an accurate measure of the character behind them, which truly counts.

I think this turns many men away from church, even though church provides an environment where a group of people engage in a mission. When we measure the strength of a church by how many people get baptized or how many dollars we donate to charity, we forsake the most important part. The mission is way out of whack.

We don't need more "success," believe it or not. Instead, we need significance.

Missions thrive when significance matters more than success. In this frame of mind, as Rocky Balboa might say, it's not about how hard you can hit; it's about how hard you can get hit and keep moving forward. Mission should be focused on the process instead of the outcome. Success is measured by how much you accumulate and get; significance takes into account your generosity—how much you give and what you're willing to endure to get there. Success is admirable, but significance is impactful.

In seeking to understand the importance of a mission in a man's life, I interviewed some incredible people. I kept waiting for someone to point to a particular cause and say, "That's where the real missions happen." The United Way. MercyShips. Habitat For Humanity. The Boys & Girls Club. The Foundation For a Better Life. But no one ever did.

These great causes brim with terrific people. But as with anything else, participating in them doesn't do you much good if you remain a mess on the inside. And the men in this chapter had plenty to say about the inside. Contrary to how the world defines it, most people who thrive with mission say it flows from within a person, and only after does it find its expression in groups and organizations.

A man on a mission fills a need where both successes and failures have value. You're in trouble if you only focus on strengths and victories. Wherever you've spent 10,000 hours establishing a track record, your mistakes, failures, and character flaws also have significant value to the people you lead.

For some men, mission can be as simple as "what you do next" when Plan A goes south. Leaders arise in all kinds of industries, sectors, and roles when events beyond our control cancel the best-laid plans.

Others find mission when they start out at rock-bottom. A popular saying encourages us to, "turn our mess into a message," and some men's missions begin after hopelessness seems like it has won the day. They face both harsh external realities and profound inner warfare. You wouldn't call them "privileged," and you can imagine how dire circumstances reduced their abilities to make good decisions.

Why aren't men thriving in mission? What's holding them back?

Missions show up in unlikely places and often require eyes of faith to bring it to life. It's easier to throw your hands up and say, "It's somebody else's job." Who wants to make provision for all the details, process and possibilities involved? Who wants to step right into a messy situation and attempt to change things for the better?

Pride blocks missions. As a younger man, I wanted to become an attorney because I wanted to be right all the time. I also wanted to earn more money than my parents did and attend Ivy League universities to get approval from people I'd never met. Some guys look at another man's mission and say, "I want to do what he does." They watch a genuine leader inspire people and admire the applause and recognition that goes with it. Many men want to be "the guy with the right answers," with crowds of followers nodding their heads in agreement.

Other men go on missions empty, hoping to "find their purpose," when what's required to thrive on a mission is to live on purpose. Be careful not to confuse mission with identity. Go and do your deep identity work first, or you'll get picked off easily in the mission field.

Then there's plain old distraction. Sometimes, we simply put mission "out of sight, out of mind." We have plenty of socially acceptable excuses: family, activities, hobbies, business and career. Not only do we have the wrong category, but we have the wrong attitude as well. Some guys just don't want to go through all that trouble. They get wrapped up in much smaller stories, like sports and hobbies. Or they're consumed by Peter Pan syndrome and sacrifice years of their lives to pursuits they should long since have outgrown—video games, partying, memorabilia and entertainment.

One way or another, the explanations and evidence for the poor male showing on mission is pride. I don't mean the swaggering, obnoxious "pride" of rock stars and Hollywood actors. This kind of pride is usually driven by fear.

We avoid missions because we live like lone wolves. We don't have people who challenge us to grow, so we shrivel and die. Our missions die with us.

We're also too prideful to believe in ourselves, ironically enough. Most men live lives of "quiet desperation," as Thoreau said, because our stories are too small. We look at significant and successful men and think, "I could never do that." Imposter syndrome sets in, and we embrace a perverse pride that masquerades as humility.

When weren't you thriving in mission?

Take a look at the cover of this book. Go ahead, I'll wait. I chose a tree on purpose. It represents the 7 Core Areas we tackled in this book. Faith and identity are the roots of the tree, sustaining everything from below. Finances, relationships, health, and career are the fruit on the branches. They show yourself and others that you're thriving, but more importantly, they bless the people in your life. Lastly, mission is the trunk. It connects the foundation of your life to the fruit. It's the conduit for your faith and identity to express themselves through your life. How connected are you to your own roots?

Dr. Bryan Hendley

As I listened to Bryan tell his story, I thought of how mission often begins in obscurity, working in jobs and tasks you hate. Think of Daniel LaRusso, washing cars and painting fences in *The Karate Kid*. He feels like a chump, trading hard labor and getting nothing in return. He's really learning the way of the warrior: hard work, discipline and sacrifice, through hours and hours of repetition. But he doesn't see it until Mr. Miyagi shows him.

Bryan didn't hate teaching, but he thought he wanted to coach kids in sports. "I knew that part at least," he said. "Many people make decisions with far less data about their mission in life, usually on the merits of what peers or mentors do. It wasn't uncommon for kids to tell me, 'I want to go to XYZ school because my mom went there,' or 'So-and-so is going, so I think I'll go too.'"

Russ Hedge

Russ is a classic example of a man minding his own business, working away diligently at "Plan B," when the ground fell out underneath him. Approaching his sixties during the recession of COVID-19, Russ realized mission was "now, or never." Like many displaced professionals, he saw the pandemic as a unique moment in history. Rarely had the world been so universally affected.

"Plan B" was in effect for Russ because "Plan A" had already failed during the previous upheaval—the Great Recession. "About ten years ago, I left a job during the darkest time of the recession," Russ told me. "They lacked vision, and there wasn't much happening there. I cared about the people there, and they didn't want to fire me . . . but they were going to have to cut me eventually because they couldn't afford to keep me on staff."

Men on mission don't hunker down and wait for the economy to improve, the pandemic to end or other external factors to 9change before they make moves. Most men, however, aren't on mission; they let themselves be controlled by factors outside their ability to influence.

Femi Doyle-Marshall

Mission came early for Femi, a young man on his way to becoming a Canadian football powerhouse when a career-ending injury torpedoed his dream. A relentless and explosive player, he transitioned into coaching in his early twenties and got swept up by the boom of the online fitness business.

He said one of the ways men manifest failure with mission is waste: "Let's take how people eat day-to-day. You're working a job or running a business, and you eat whatever you can find to survive. This is an example of creating and storing waste inside your body. On a spiritual level, guys do exactly the same thing."

So what's the correlation? Should we interpret our poor physical shape as a sign of poor psychological shape?

"That depends on how seriously men take their responsibilities," Femi replied, "and on where they get their wisdom. Are they getting it from books or from Facebook? Are they having the kind of conversations that lead them to behaving responsibly, or are they just talking about sports and the weather?"

We can probably answer that, can't we? Isn't it so easy to stay in the superficial level of life? We can have a casual conversation about the weather or making money, but how does that transform anything?

By Femi's account, this mindset deterred his mission, the "Reboot" Academy, from reaching its potential. "In my first business, it was all about outcomes," he admitted. "The money side worked. But I lost focus, drive and purpose. I slacked on caring for my own soul. Lack of mission created a huge gap in my life. I became depressed, suicidal and focused on vanity metrics . . . and none of it made me feel any better."

This man was running a successful seven-figure business! On the surface, that would qualify as a "mission," wouldn't it? If you're attracting enough clients to earn over a million dollars from fitness coaching, doesn't that count as strong leadership?

How many miserable millionaires do we need to read about before we learn this: It's not about the money.

Okay, I'll get off the soap box. But Femi eventually succumbed to a stress attack and landed in the hospital for several weeks. During his stay, he had trouble walking with coordination and talking coherently. His wife, Winnie, had to ask him to promise her he'd never let himself get that bad again.

Shane Sams

Mission can also come from a catastrophic moment that feels like a direct assault on identity, as it did for Shane. He, too, was on his way to playing football—and got sideswiped by a career-ending injury. Unable to participate directly, Shane attempted the next best thing: coaching high school athletes. But impostor syndrome quickly set in, and Shane felt the stinging insecurity from his inability to teach students from his own experience.

He kept fighting harder, attending grad school to fill himself with enough knowledge to prove his value. He quit his coaching job and became an online entrepreneur, selling playbooks and coaching products. But impostor syndrome surfaced there, too. He could not get free until he learned to reject damaging assumptions about how his mission was supposed to look.

"I felt under-qualified because I wasn't succeeding," Shane said. "I started copying elite coaches like [University of Alabama head coach] Nick Saban. The problem was I wasn't working with players of the same caliber, so a lot of what I taught simply didn't apply. But my interpretation was that I'd failed as a coach. I became very good at the comparison trap."

Nate Dukes

Can you thrive on mission even if your life generally resembles a raw deal? Nate Dukes grew up in chaos and dysfunction. His parents, he told me, were "kids trying to raise kids." They passed on several broken beliefs and attitudes. Nate wanted to escape the pain of his upbringing and bought into the notion that money, power, and success would give him the way out. If people simply perceived Nate as "the man," everything else would take care of itself.

By the time he reached his teenage and young adult years, Nate's dream began to take a turn for the worse. Alcohol and drugs interfered with college. He had to take medicine to focus, which led him down the path of harder drugs. Soon, what was once a "weekend thing" became a full-blown addiction. Nate failed to earn a degree and had to move back in with his parents.

Along with some friends, Nate purchased a failing local bar and turned it into a successful one. "All of a sudden, I had access to more money than I'd ever seen in my life," he said. "I had a good car, a nice apartment and I thought it would make me happy. When it didn't, I countered by trying to acquire even more stuff—which led me into gambling. I went from drug and alcohol addiction to gambling, and eventually gambled away everything I had. Then I started stealing money from the business' accounts to the point I gambled away our employees' payroll money."

Sadly, Nate's story didn't end there. He exited the business and moved back in with his parents, where he resumed abusing drugs. He drifted for a while, going from one job to the next, stealing from employers and getting fired. Finally, in an attempt to run away and start over, Nate stole a car from his parents' apartment complex. He drove all night until he was too tired to continue and woke up to the window-knocking of a state trooper on the side of a highway. He spent the following six months in jail.

How can you go from failure to thriving in mission?

Mission starts by learning to ask the right questions instead of knowing the right answers. You stop trying to gain moral authority over others. Instead, you yearn for truth, wisdom, and self-awareness. You don't go on a mission to acquire "more." You're grateful for what you have because you know that things you appreciate tend to appreciate themselves. If there's "more" to gain with mission, it means giving more.

John D. Rockefeller described success as "the pursuit of more," but significance is more likely to be found in what Dr. Viktor Frankl called the "search for meaning"—a clear conviction that your life matters and impacts the lives of others around you.

What does it look like to thrive in mission?

Bryan's mission unfolded when he flipped the script on a specific problem. He thought his mission was to improve a player's jump-shot. But where they truly needed help was with life-altering, long-lasting decisions about future, education, and career. "I started sharing things like the Purpose Project with adults," Bryan said. "Ninety-nine times out of a hundred, people raised their hands and said they needed it. So I thought, 'Why can't we offer the same kind of thing for young people?'"

Over years of counseling students about their futures, the law of 10,000 hours kicked in. Bryan began to see flaws and weaknesses in the decisions students often made before they told him. Like predictive text, he could guess what these students were thinking based on the fragments they shared. He discovered basketball had only been the bait to draw him into a story of much greater significance. "I was committed to doing a good job, so I began to ask, 'How can we create a decision-making framework for students . . . to make a good decision, based on what matters most to them?'" He started his own coaching program designed to help young people map out their future in alignment with their dreams.

Russ turned the collapse of his career into a new business as a marketing consultant. His book serves as a helpful reminder of how mission isn't necessarily defined by nonprofit status, church affiliation or religious branding. Russ wrote a book called *Befuddled? Live the Life You Choose.* "I knew I had to get that book out as soon as possible," he told me. "It contained a message people needed to hear for everything we went through. More and more people needed to find purpose to get through all the chaos."

Femi spent a long season of discontent with his former business, New Persona Fitness, until he evolved into his current entrepreneurial offering RebootX Academy. "I had a lease renewal coming up for New Persona," he said, "and the landlord suddenly went nuts. We didn't renew the lease. Then the pandemic hit—and the whole world went upside-down. Two months later, I backed out of a new lease agreement and shut New Persona down." Shut down a seven-figure business?

"There's more than one way to eliminate waste," he replied. "You can do it with relationships, family, finances or spiritual matters. The waste is going to get in your way. You have to be nimble because you're going to face obstacles and challenges." All those years of studying patterns, as an athlete and coach, gave Femi the ability to notice and identify destructive patterns in his own life. New Persona, the business that had skyrocketed and caused Femi to "reboot" his own thinking, had stuck him in a holding pattern.

"When you can distinguish between positive and negative patterns, there's only one decision left to make," Femi added. "Choose more and more positive patterns more often. I learned to start with rituals—systems and structures for each day, start to finish. I observe patterns from people I want to emulate, and then I create my own versions. And I always make sure they align with my identity."

If we started to set up rituals and patterns like Femi describes, would our missions do the same thing? Would they gravitate to us, so we wouldn't have to chase them?

Nate Dukes' long fall began to turn around when he realized the two biggest factors in the mission of a man's life are the choices he makes and the voices he listens to while making them. "The right voices lead to the right choices," he said. "I use the 'Rule of Five.' If you're the average of the five people you spend the most time with, you should start to notice the 'fruit' in their lives. If you don't want the fruit they're producing, don't take their advice." From my personal experience participating in masterminds, I couldn't agree more.

Is thriving in mission worth it?

We don't have to wait for a life-altering event to wake us up to the larger story. We can manufacture our own wake-up calls, if we can do the dirty work upfront.

Now is the time. Be an actor, not a reactor. Stop over-thinking this and get started. We spend too much time planning, muddling and worrying and we never get anything done. Once you know your mission, it's time to act.

Take time away from all the noise and distractions, so you can answer tough questions for yourself. Study the scriptures, wrestle with them, and make room for them to influence your decisions and thoughts about your mission.

Begin with the end in mind. If you know who you are and what you want, you can also begin to describe how you'd like to be remembered. You can visualize the impact you have on the world and reverse-engineer steps to get there.

The vision you have is worth it. Negative feelings disappear when you learn to operate in the invisible. It will give you life when you pause, rethink, reboot and eliminate waste. Your mission will have a paycheck, but more than that, it will have purpose.

Additionally, "mission" does not equal "picnic." We must reject comfort, embrace hardship, endure affliction and persevere in prayer. Be prepared to stumble, fail and be misunderstood on your mission. It goes with the territory of living on purpose.

Most of all, we have to believe it, deep down inside. We can't afford to fall prey to our own sense of unworthiness, or mistake the heart and character of God to think He's against us.

Reminder: This book was designed to help you in the areas you need it most. If you're reading straight through, great! Keep going. If you're reading this chapter because you took the assessment and now want to jump to the last chapter instead of tackling other Core Areas, go ahead!

You can find additional resources for mission by listening to the Made to Thrive *podcast episodes featuring these men, or by visiting amithriving.com*

Chapter Four:

RELATIONSHIPS

I n this chapter, we'll focus on three different kinds of relationships, unique and distinct from each other: marriage, fatherhood and brotherhood.

Would you like to know what they all have in common? All of your relationships are either growing—or dying. You can't really have a permanently fixed connection between two people. It will always lead toward greater connection or death. The closer you bond or connect to someone, the more this rule applies.

Here's another thing: Relational quality serves as a barometer for how you score across all 7 Core Areas. How likely are you to be a great husband and father if you don't have a good connection with friendships and community? For example, a poor life at home affects how you relate to everybody at work.

Some of the big problems we discovered for men in relationships include:

1. Too many guys wait for the other person to make a change.
2. Men are mission-driven (point A to point B), but relationships aren't linear.
3. Men think relationships are a lot of work, when they aren't.
4. Society measures men's relationships one-dimensionally (i.e., "husband" = "provider").
5. Relational mastery isn't taught well; like a math teacher gifted in math, most relational 'experts' simply assume you understand what they mean the first time.

We have our work cut out for us, so let's get to it.

RELATIONSHIPS PART ONE: MARRIAGE

A successful marriage requires falling in love many times, always with the same person.
— Mignon McLaughlin

To be fully seen by somebody, then, and loved anyhow—this is a human offering that can border on miraculous.
— Elizabeth Gilbert

How would you rate your marriage? Is it lousy, mediocre, "good, but it could be better," or great? Few men tie the knot hoping for anything other than the last option. But, if I could be so bold to try to narrate what the average young groom hopes as he stands at the altar, it might go something like this:

Yay, now I get to have sex with my biggest fan every day!

Okay, maybe that's a little oversimplified. Plus, our young groom has one thing right: If a woman agrees to marry you, she doesn't think you're the least attractive guy in the room. Exclusive sexual access and her admiration certainly form part of the equation. However, many newlywed husbands view their wedding day as something akin to conquering a mountain. "Been there, done that, what's next?"

If we're being honest, you've just reached the trailhead.

Why aren't men thriving in marriage? What's holding them back?

Marriage gives us quite a bit to do, it turns out. Most men have no idea what they just got themselves into. Even if you're fortunate enough to have someone who can explain it to you, marriage is a journey to discover the unique heart of your bride. Not long after their wedding days, men find themselves bewildered by their wives. At varying speeds, many find themselves settling into marriages that are, well, lousy, mediocre or "good, but could be better."

When weren't you thriving in marriage?

As I mentioned in the introduction, the first few years of my marriage were rough. I had to learn quite a bit the hard way, usually through my own pride or foolishness. It wasn't supposed to be that way; after all, we did premarital counseling like all good Christian couples are supposed to. The only problem? It was all theory and no context, so the principles flew out the window when we were met with real life. I wish I knew these guys back then.

Evan Money

A career entrepreneur, coach, speaker and filmmaker, Evan Money came from what he calls a "normal, dysfunctional family." He saw how marriage worked with his and his friends' parents. He didn't want any part of it. But what were the alternatives? Evan didn't know anyone who thrived in marriage.

"Growing up, I noticed there were three options," he said. "'Married and Miserable,' 'Single and Cynical' or 'Divorced and Desperate.' I wasn't interested in those, so I began to read whatever I could get my hands on to figure out how to avoid what seemed inevitable for everyone else." Evan knew enough to defy fear of failure, which stops men from growing. His journey reveals how men fail in marriage due to a lack of awareness of what's possible or available.

"Happiness isn't some magical 'place' to be discovered," he said. "It's a reality to be created every day with your bride. But is that what you see in your average church? Do you see anyone running around promoting a thriving marriage with great sex between two firmly committed people who love each other?" We don't need to answer the question. What do most church marriage retreats and seminars focus on? It looks and sounds more like damage control, if you ask me. An example of what Dallas Willard called "the gospel of sin management."

Here's another interesting point Evan brought up: Most men find themselves "sexually empty."

"We can't give what we don't have," he explained, "so we give a deformed and limited version of 'love.' Our integrity is compromised because we associate doing difficult things with pain, which we want to avoid. Often, you'll hear men say things like, 'I have to do such and such.' That's the language of an emotional handicap. These guys are 'takers' in the bedroom, but

not 'givers' in the home. And their identity is also compromised: They think one-dimensionally about their
role as a husband." That sounds familiar; "husband"
equals "provider."

Nick Matiash

Similar problems surfaced for Nick, a career educator
who coaches men in marriage. Early on, he lacked the
vulnerability and the courage to disclose his unhappiness
to his wife. "Men usually enter marriage with very little
in the way of emotional depth," he said. "We're crippled
in our understanding and capacity to deal with our own
emotions. And so, we're even less equipped to deal with
the women we love."

I wonder, if that's the case, what does it say about the
historical, societal narrative that women are "more emotional" than men? Some say it's exactly the opposite, and
I'm inclined to agree, especially if you look at men's behavior when they lose control of themselves.

"We have a natural tendency to think we know
and understand everything, or at least feel pressure to
act like we do," Nick added. "We think we can 'power
through' anything that comes up and end up making ourselves into martyrs." That one stung. I know I've done
my fair share of "sacrificial" things for Marita, while
underneath I was seething or feeling sorry for myself.
What is it with us that refuses to engage in true kindness
and sacrificial love?

Seth Studley

Clarity is another marriage "homework assignment" most men fail to complete, according to Seth Studley. Together with his wife, Melanie, Seth counsels men and couples. They primarily do coaching and marriage/family therapy. Like Nick, Seth observes that men simply fear broaching certain subjects with their wives.

What drives this? What makes men, supposedly the more direct and blunt of the two sexes, suddenly turn into obsequious diplomats, or silent, seething grudge-holders? Seth referred me to the perennial problem presented by John Eldredge in *Wild At Heart*: All men want to know, "Do I have what it takes?" For many, that question remains unanswered. We live in marriages driven by fear because we feel uncertain of ourselves.

Seth ended up with a literal black eye to jolt him out of hitting the "snooze" button on authenticity in his marriage to Melanie. "She asked me, about eight years into the marriage, if I ever looked at pornography," Seth said. "At first I denied it, but lying to my wife really bugged me. So I confessed that I occasionally did." She slugged him in the face and came dangerously close to leaving him.

How can you go from failure to thriving in marriage?

What would it look like for men to stop dismissing their own emotions as "feminine," and develop a healthy degree of fluency and versatility with them? We need to stop dodging hard conversations and quit "powering through" the inevitable sense of disappointment and victimhood that come from keeping silent? The pathway to a poor marriage lies in sweeping things under the rug and pretending everything's okay, more so than in obvious offenses like abuse or having an affair.

Men place unrealistic expectations on their wives to remain the way they appear on the wedding day—young, beautiful, vivacious, childless and care-free. Can you accept that the woman you love will be different five years down the road? It's the same as she is now, when compared with five years ago: different. Do you believe you will be different in five years? "You'd better hope she's different," said Evan.

It's inevitable: the people you love will change. Why do we expect anything else? The better questions are, "How would you describe the change you'd like to see?" and "Who do you have the most power to change for the better?"

Evan had an intriguing illustration: Find life-giving things you can pursue, both as individuals and together, besides children. "Life is like a river," he said. "If you and your bride decide to join your rafts together, that's great, but you're still two distinct, separate beings. And the thing about rivers is they drift. They have currents. The drift will overpower and pull you apart if you don't paddle together."

Yikes. That sounds like a lot of work, particularly with someone so fundamentally different. But people do it all the time, and not just because the stars align or their horoscopes and personalities match. Some simply refuse to give up. They keep digging until they strike gold.

For Seth, the low point in his marriage led to the break-through. "At the very least, I knew that I got married for better reasons than using pornography and lying about it. There had to be more, and we resolved together to work through everything." Although Seth and Melanie went through a trying season, they soon discovered the world was full of other couples who needed their help. They began to pull back the curtain on everything in coaching programs and on their *Marriage, Family, Sex* podcast. It became more than a breakthrough: It turned into a way of life and a business.

What does it look like to thrive in marriage?
The men answered unanimously: Put yourself in constant growth mode.

"As much as I've learned about people and relation-ships, I've learned never to think that I've learned every-thing there is to know," said Nick. "I learned to ask my wife, 'What do you need from me?' While I'm very good at explaining and clarifying what I need from her, it never occurred to me to turn the question in the other direction."

What else would any woman conclude if you never ask? It's probably the same as what she'd conclude if you never asked her to marry you: It isn't that important to him. It's staggering how often men think our silence means the same thing to a wife as it does to another man.

Evan suggested we live our lives like parables. Men have a knack for discerning formulas, but not parables. They never tell you what the outcomes are. Jesus deliberately left them open. "Did the prodigal son get fully restored to his family?" Evan asked. "Did his brother drop his grudge and join the party? We don't really know the answers." Each outcome of a parable is unique to the participants.

The Moneys do not take their cues from other couples; they create their own. They have an incredible story of getting remarried each year, frequently in exotic locations. They've done it all twenty-four years they've been together (Dubai is the next locale). "I live a newlywed lifestyle," Evan said. "At any moment, I'm either in post-honeymoon bliss or planning a new wedding." No wonder he refers to Susan exclusively as "his bride." What else do you call a woman you just married or are just about to marry?

Marriages also require unifying interests, such as Nick and his wife's shared passion for entrepreneurship. "I coach men. My wife, meanwhile, is a makeup artist for weddings," he told me. "That gives us a lot to talk about together, and we also enjoy 'me time,' without having to be a dad or a mom." Do you both love to play a sport or a hobby? Do you enjoy certain kinds of entertainment or educational subjects? In his book, *Happily Ever After*, Evan tells the story of winning Susan's reciprocity by watching TV shows she likes. Yes, this does mean appreciating and giving your attention to the feminine world. It won't kill you, and you won't have to turn in your "man card." I promise.

Seth's journey to the brink of marital failure revealed just how strong he could become—not through willpower, mind you, but through habits. "I can always look back at certain stages in my life when I had systems or habits in place," he said, "and compare it against the opposite. If there's a difference in the quality of life, then it's about picking up good habits and staying consistent. I tell people, 'Do what you know you're capable of doing and do it more often. Be open to new things. Show up with the right intentions. Keep to agreements and schedules."

Wait, you mean we should treat our wives with the same respect and openness we show to friends, co-workers and complete strangers? I'm fairly sure, if we looked up a definition of "love," this would qualify as an example.

Is thriving in marriage worth it?
It isn't easy to find an exemplary couple, but they're out there. You can have a thriving marriage. You can do it, and it's easier than you might think. And the benefits of growing this relationship spill over into the others. There's a lot of truth to the classic saying, "Happy wife, happy life."

The reverse is also true, by the way: "Happy life, happy wife." If your life is constantly growing and thriving, your wife will find you inspiring, attractive, worth following, and great in bed. It's nature's law, not Sam Feeney's.

If you've failed to thrive in marriage and long periods of neglect and deterioration have buried your relationship, you can still take hope. Forgive yourself and refuse to carry shame and guilt. Don't go through life thinking you're "damaged goods" or "too far gone." Learn to forgive and release your former self and decide instead who you want to become. Write down how you want to show up and what kind of man you want to be.

Seth created an acronym P.I.G.G.S.—which stands for Prayer, Intentions, Gratitude, Goals, and Service—toward your wife.

Pray for her. If there's one thing the spiritual leader of a home is meant to do, it's this.

Think well of her, the intentions you have toward her, and how you'd like her to feel about being married to you.

Be **grateful** for her and everything she does. And make certain she knows how you feel.

Share your **goals** and dreams with her and invite her into them. Make her a co-author of your life story

Finally, **serve** her the way she wants to be served.

Reminder: This book was designed to help you in the areas you need it most. If you're reading straight through, great! Keep going. If you're reading this chapter because you took the assessment and now want to jump to the last chapter instead of tackling other Core Areas, go ahead!

RELATIONSHIPS PART TWO: FATHERHOOD

You have many teachers, but not many fathers.
— **The Apostle Paul**

If there is any immortality to be had among us human beings, it is certainly only in the love that we leave behind. Fathers like mine don't ever die.
— **Leo Buscaglia**

Of the hats we wear as men, none of them has anything like the capacity to affect or impact the world—for better or worse—as "father."

Think of it this way: Imagine that you were the father of one of the world's most influential people in history. Take your pick of good or evil. Joan of Arc, Adolf Hitler, Winston Churchill, Mahatma Gandhi, Mother Teresa, Genghis Khan and Napoleon Bonaparte. Every single one of these people had a father who impacted them *somehow.*

Were these fathers good, bad, or indifferent? Maybe some were great, but their kids turned out horribly. Perhaps some were evil, yet their kids turned out to be great. No one knows the future of the helpless infant in your hands on the day they come into the world. And you have no idea how their presence will change things for you. But you can make decisions and do something about the man holding the helpless infant, the guy who will have a huge impact on them.

In the journey of exploration and discovery to understand thriving as a father, I kept thinking of the title of Simon Sinek's 2019 book, *The Infinite Game*. I didn't understand why its title rang so relevant to the topic of fatherhood.

Then it hit me: How much do we, as men, feel the weight of our own fathers (and ancestors) in our lives? How often do we lean on the examples they provided, the societies and cultures they built, and the momentum their lives gave (or failed to give) to ours?

If that's true, how much more do we, parenting kids today, need to take a closer look at how our actions and decisions affect them? The data confirms it over and again: We possess incredible power to build or destroy our kids' lives.

A man's identity plays a huge role in this area. We have to stop treating the word "provider" as a suitable definition of "father." No one qualifies as a good father just because he can pay the bills. How tragically oversimplified; "He's an abusive alcoholic and womanizer, but at least we can pay the bills!"

Here's another travesty: We don't teach men to communicate well. Men's voices and words alter the directions of entire lives. The best our culture can manage is to tell men what we should not say, rather than model how a man should speak. Many of us obey them, keeping silent and failing to nourish our kids in the process.

We have yet to recover from the separation between fathers and children caused by the Industrial Revolution and two World Wars. Robert Bly, in his book *Iron John*, noted that the traditional way of raising sons included years together (decades, sometimes) of a son learning a trade at a father's side. But by the time you and I came along, this practice was history. Fathers today spend more time at work (away from their children) than with them.

The bar for success as a father today is set fairly low. The world has so many poor or absent fathers that by merely sticking around, you meet much of the criteria. But that's the old "Hippocratic Oath" thing coming back again. Who wants to simply "exist" in our kids' lives? Isn't there more to life than having a pulse?

I kept hearing my wife's question: "Is this all there is?" along with a nagging sensation that the answer is "No." So, how can we begin to reframe this part of a man's life?

Why aren't men thriving as fathers? What's holding them back?

An inadequate father—absent, abusive, passive or otherwise destructive—is inherently ill-suited for the task of raising a child from birth to young adulthood. Unless he grows and matures himself, he becomes a ticking time bomb. At some point, something will go wrong.

But even dads who are present, constructive, engaged and growth-oriented fail you somewhere. Even if you grew up with an outstanding father in your home, somewhere, somehow, he came up short. The adversity might affect you less severely, but it does affect you. It impacts us all. There's nothing wrong with acknowledging that.

When weren't you thriving in fatherhood?

Tell me if you've heard this one before. I took a parenting class at church, and on the second night, I started to get really scared. Whenever the teacher asked a question, it was always answered by me or one other man there. It felt self-conscious to be doing so well in this parenting class. What did myself and this other genius have in common? We were the only expecting fathers in the class. Everyone else already had kids. In other words, we were the best fathers ever—until the kids actually arrived, and blew our fancy theories out of the water. I needed to talk to some men whose principles for fatherhood have actually stood the test of fatherhood.

Blake Brewer

On a sunny, warm and tropical afternoon on the beaches of Hawaii, Blake Brewer went through the harrowing nightmare of losing a loving, kind, strong and successful father. Larry Brewer died in a terrible drowning accident. Larry was a career athlete, including a stint as a tight end for Terry Bradshaw during the Pittsburgh Steelers' heyday in the 1970s.

I can't imagine the magnitude of such an event on a nineteen-year-old boy, who only moments before had felt safe, loved and prized. "I went from having the time of my life on a family vacation, with us all together in paradise, soaking up the best of what life has to offer, to being father-less," Blake said. "It was the best day of my life and the worst day of my life. It felt surreal, as though we were in a movie, and he would wake up any minute."

But it never happened. Larry was gone.

Omar Barlow

Omar grew up with a strong, loving father who gave him the nickname "Big O." He never cared much about the amount of money his father earned; it was his presence that was enriching. Omar credits his dad for helping him develop securely in his identity, meet challenges, and suc-cessfully marry his wife and raise his own children. But many kids grow up without their dads, and Omar acknowl-edged quickly the strains and internal chaos it causes.

As the CEO and principal of Eastern University Academy Charter School, Omar spent a decade interact-ing with hundreds of children. He's seen firsthand how deeply the craving runs for affirmation from male author-ity figures. "You start to discern what people are crying out for," he said. "You see it over and over: People want their fathers to speak for them and about them. They want to be in the presence of their dads and hear a voice of affirmation and identity.

"Boys especially grow tired of hearing their mother's voice," he continued. "There's no 'counter-voice' for a mother's voice. They become angry and resentful of mom, whereas people who grow up hearing their father's voice tend to have a lot more peace."

Do you understand the enormous power you wield simply in your voice? What about the authority and weight you carry with your kids the moment your mouth begins to move? When I heard Omar's conviction, I've got to be honest, I didn't previously attach that degree of importance to how I speak to my kids.

Isolated upbringings and stunted spirituality limit a man's ability to understand their children's spiritual nature. Many guys never see other men doing the things that lead to thriving. A lack of solid masculine examples leads to a lack of solid masculine men. Whether it's because we've ceded an unfair proportion of leadership to women, failed to provide space to share struggles or don't know how to make life work in balance, we fail to thrive and model dysfunction in the process.

Thomas Paine once said that men "esteem too lightly what they obtain too cheaply." Think about it: Physically, our wives go through a much more tangible and experiential process of bringing our kids into the world than we do. We get "ringside seats" to the occasion and a lifetime of responsibility, but we have no physical changes or scars embedded on our bodies as reminders (other than the occasional right hook from our wives during childbirth).

Maybe it's time we thought more deeply about the consequences of our words and actions, even if they're honorable and noble. We occupy a privileged position of deep, lasting impact. Don't discount or downplay it.

Jon Vroman

Jon mentioned our most constant problem: Pride. Men simply don't see how much pride and ego get in our way. We have no clue how quickly our defensive walls go up when someone takes us to task about our failures. "Do you have a growth mindset or a fixed one?" Jon asked. "Can you look at the opposite perspective and consider that it might be true? What if it is? Enlightenment is what allows us to change conversations and questions."

Men understand the need to develop and improve at work. We need to do better, learn more, take more responsibility and smarter risks. We understand that our success and position are correlated with our efforts and commitment. Why don't we understand this at home? Could this even be true for fathers, even if your kids are grown up and having kids themselves?

Perhaps you can't get your adult daughter's childhood back, but you can certainly improve how you relate to her as a grown woman. You may have blown it with your son in his teens, but you can still change how you handle him now.

Or maybe you withheld discipline for your own kids and let them do as they pleased growing up. You may not be able to reach them, but you could teach your hard-earned wisdom to other people's children. Young people all over the world need someone wise to teach them things they can't find on Google, such as:

1. "Actions have consequences."
2. "There's a way the world works."
3. "Love is a verb, not a feeling."
4. "If you say 'Yes' to one thing, you say 'No' to something else."

How can you go from failure to thriving in fatherhood?

Hours after his father's death, Blake wrestled with loss and grief while calling family members, friends and associates to inform them of Larry's passing. His mother brought him an envelope from her suitcase. It contained a letter from Larry to his three children, written just months before his death. "It was meant to be a gift he planned to give to me during the trip," Blake explained. "I opened it and found the most heartfelt, genuine and detailed words from my dad to us. I had never felt so loved and cared for."

The letter proved so pivotal that Blake went on to found *The Legacy Letter*, a course he now offers to fathers in organizations around the world. Professional teams and corporate firms began to license the letter as a team-building exercise.

Larry Brewer has been gone for eighteen years, but death has not silenced him. It hasn't silenced your dad or mine, either. Our fathers still speak to us. This bold move, ahead of an untimely death, led ultimately to a movement spearheaded by Larry's son.

Omar was overwhelmed when he started Eastern Academy University Charter School. After a decade of involvement, he realized he'd been in way over his head. "I have painful experiences," he said. "I made it hard for my family because they didn't have access to me. It weakened our relationships. The pandemic actually saved us because it forced us to slow down, talk and actually live together. All the ways we should have been working together *finally* began to work."

I found that eye-opening. A lot of relationships got hammered by the COVID-19 pandemic when people could no longer hit "snooze" on the hard work by staying distracted. How do you deal with loving your family when you suddenly spend far more time with them than you ever have? It was a challenge in the Feeney home, with a house of five kids, mostly under age ten.

Jon went down a similar path to Omar. He wrote a book called *Front Row Factor* while working intensely on the Front Row Foundation, a nonprofit he founded. He got caught in the "charity trap"—an eager desire to "make a difference." But the only difference that mattered was the rift Jon created between himself and his wife. "She pulled me aside one day," Jon confessed, "and told me, 'You've been more of a moment maker with that foundation than you have with your own family!'"

Ouch. Have you ever got into trouble with your family for doing the right thing—or at least, what you thought was the right thing? Have you ever lost yourself in another core area, like mission, at the expense of your most important relationships?

What does it look like to thrive in fatherhood?

Blake's Legacy Letter process offers a prime example of the power of journaling and scripting, which we teach in Made To Thrive mastermind groups.

"When you sit down and begin to write out the ways your father failed you, it does something incredible," Blake said. "You develop an earnestness to avoid his mistakes. So, if he was absent, you start to think of all the ways you want to be present. If he was passive, you think of how you want to be active and engaged."

Thriving has a script, in other words, and we get to write it. Blake's letter shows how, by putting pen to paper, you take these thoughts out of the deep recesses of your memory and make them active and powerful agents to propel you toward thriving. Blake added, "It helps you thrive as a father because you have vision for your family. You choose to be present with them. Your kids can feel when you're there, listening and engaging with them."

Omar said conversations with your family will show you if you really value the relationship with them like you say you do. Can you talk to them? Do they reciprocate? If not, it's a good sign they don't feel close to you like they should.

Omar pointed to Jesus as the King modeling the King-dom. "What does it look like to live a royal, godly life?" he asked. "One thing you need to do is spend quality time with God because you need to heal and grow to be at peace. You need to model this to your kids and let them see you care for your own soul. And you need healthy friendships with the right kind of people, so your kids can see what kind of men you hang around."

Jon agreed. "Thriving men spend a lot of time with their kids and offer more compliments than criticism. They give from a thriving core, and you can tell because their wives and children thrive as well. They take care of themselves and their health, which gives them the energy and drive to put their families ahead of themselves."

Is thriving in fatherhood worth it?

Success and significance as a father aren't always easy to measure. Often, what you sow into your kids' lives may remain dormant for decades until the season they need it. Or it might show up, but you don't recognize it because it looks different than you expected. Depending on where you are, you may have some apologies to make to your kids. Make them directly, wholeheartedly and authentically. Your ability to be unconditionally apologetic is a sign of strength and trustworthiness to them—not weakness.

And one thing's clear: It is oh-so-totally worth it.

"Who wants to be on their deathbed surrounded by co-workers commenting on how much money you earned while working with them?" Blake snorted. "Not me! I want my family around me, telling me how much my life meant to them."

With training, knowledge, and community, you can find the capacity to become a great father. Don't look at your development as a dad as something weird, new-age or feminine. This is an act of manly force. We need to take fatherhood back. When you change, the entire environment around you will yield.

Fathering is an infinite game. Unlike a sports contest, where there's a clear winner and loser when the clock runs out, we make moves and call plays that project well beyond our lives, as well as those of our children and grandchildren. What we do in life, as Maximus said in *Gladiator*, "echoes in eternity."

You've probably heard that once you're a parent, you're always a parent. Just because those little crumb-crunchers eventually grow up and fly the coop doesn't mean you stop being their dad. You're just at a new level of the role with far less hands-on work.

So, let's not let our current circumstances control us. Instead, let's pledge ourselves to intentionality as a lifestyle and surround ourselves with like-minded fathers to challenge us and hold us accountable.

I'm in if you are.

Reminder: This book was designed to help you in the areas you need it most. If you're reading straight through, great! Keep going. If you're reading this chapter because you took the assessment and now want to jump to the last chapter instead of tackling other Core Areas, go ahead!

RELATIONSHIPS PART THREE: BROTHERHOOD

If you find yourself weak in persistence, surround
yourself with a mastermind group."
— Napoleon Hill

You are the average of the five people you spend
the most time with.
— Jim Rohn

Humans require life-giving friendships, more than we often admit. Still, almost everyone has them, but not everyone thrives with them. We'd be wise to modify by pursuing friendships that are growing, generous, powerful and dynamic. That's what most men really need. But we settle for far less.

The cultural caricature of male-to-male relationships gives us a short-term outlook, usually around the topics of cars, sports, entertainment or their "glory days" in high school and college. It's all but inevitable, especially among a group of men who don't know each other well. Many men's relationships quickly fizzle into transactional rather than transformational. We tend to prioritize other things (money, possessions, and pride) more than depth, intimacy, and transparency.

Then we have the internal baggage we bring into our public life: The tone and content of how we think of ourselves reflected in the words we speak. We don't see ourselves clearly. Much of what we say comes across differently to others than we assume. If you've struggled to be a likable guy, remember: You are the most common factor of all your relationships. We always have room for growth.

If a man feels dissatisfied with his friends and acquaintances or with friendship in general, he must be prepared to look in the mirror. No relationship will work well unless you also work well. But it's not just you. Millions of men around the world find themselves in the same (or worse) shape. We're passive (at best) about who gains access to our lives. We had a time when friendship was as simple as racing tricycles, but those days are gone.

Men don't do "homework" on the choices available to them. The truth is, there are plenty of people, in a vastly interconnected world, with whom you can build ties. If the local scene truly doesn't cut it, there's no sense spinning your wheels and blaming others.

Why aren't men thriving in brotherhood? What's holding them back?

They don't teach us how to relate to others in school. At least, until not until we get into trouble. Even then, it only corrects the worst behavior instead of demonstrating positive behavior. A young boy spends a lot of time in school learning what he should not do, what's not okay, and what gets him into trouble. As we know, most of it goes in one ear and out the other.

You can't find virtuous "masculine behavior" and "friendships of honor" in the curriculum. The Industrial Revolution reshaped the teaching profession into one dominated by women, which limits boys' exposure to positive male examples.

Classical, dignified treatment of women as "ladies" is out of style. All a boy learns now is how he may not behave. More and more ground disappears, until today's schoolboys find themselves standing on a tiny shred of territory labeled "what will keep me out of trouble."

I'll say it again: Every time you say "Yes" to one thing, you say "No" to something else. We've said "no" to an awful lot of things that used to be distinctly masculine and good. But has it brought us any closer to a world where we behave more like men and less like animals? By saying "No" to ways we used to sharpen, challenge and refine one another, have we disrupted the "supply chain" of principled, virtuous manly living from one generation of men to the next?

One about masculinity doesn't change: It is bestowed, as John Eldredge says. Boys do not become men through simple biological processes alone. They can't be made into men by women, and they can't be initiated by peers. They need men—stronger, wiser, selfless and committed men— to show up, so they can grow up.

When weren't you thriving in brotherhood?

To be frank, brotherhood was one of my weakest areas going into the formation of this book. I'm really good at transactional relationships. You do this, I say this, we shake hands and part ways. I'm not very good at transformational relationships. They require time, energy, and vulnerability. Who has an excess of any of those to spare for brotherhood? However, I knew the lack of community in this area was hurting me. So, I was very excited to start figuring it out.

Adam Connors

When Adam joined *Made To Thrive*, he argued the same concept from a business perspective: Bestowing masculinity goes way beyond flipping a switch. "No one plays the 'long game,'" he said. "We like to make the excuse that we're 'busy,' but the truth is, relationships aren't a priority. They're transactional, not transformational."

Adam believes men could get far more of what they want, much more often than they do, by learning to network. A career entrepreneur who's owned companies in diverse industries, he now leads an educational company called NetWorkWise, which teaches people personal and professional growth through the power of quality relationships. It comes from decades of experience building, scaling and leading a multitude of different organizations.

Luciano Del Monte

With a career, marriage and ministry spanning four decades, Luciano (also known as "Luch") enriched our conversation about community by bringing along two of his closest friends, Steph Pettersson and Dean Allison.

Luch entered ministry shortly after marrying his wife, Rosetta. Early on, he had a father's heart for younger men, including his own three sons. He built some of his closest and most enduring friendships through the "Mavericks," a men's group he leads, among whom Steph and Dean are members.

Luch says men learn wrongly that "life in the Body of Christ is 'one-on-one'—just you and God. It's sort of like saying that golf is all about putting. Clearly, there's more to it than that. This one-to-one idea contradicts Scripture; God is in the habit of using the people closest to us to sharpen, correct, confront and comfort us."

But what goes on in the modern Western church? It doesn't seem like showing up to church or Bible study does enough to give us solid brotherhood. We've made it all about rules and appearances. No wonder men see right through it and don't want any part of it. I've played that game. Have you ever told people in church, "I'm fine," because you don't want them to know what's really going on? Or worse, have you said it because you think they don't care?

Warren Peterson

As the founder of Significant Man Ministries, Warren has a mission to bring together men who feel sick of life in the shallow end. And that includes the shallow ends in churches, business and any other human institution.

In Warren's case, the marketplace became the first arena. "I placed all the burdens of my questions and identity on a business I co-owned with my wife," he told me. "Everything depended on its success or failure: My income, her job, our mortgage. If it failed, so did we."

And they did fail. "We lost absolutely everything," Warren continued. "I struggled with deep depression and contemplated suicide. And one reason was that I faced it alone. Many men in Western culture don't have friendships that get much beyond talking about sports or cars. They may not even realize they need these connections until something catastrophic happens."

How can you go from failure to thriving in brotherhood?

We'll always have men who want to talk about beer, cars, sports and surface-level issues. But you won't find those conversations very life-giving. There's a paradigm shift coming: You need to become more selective and intentional regarding whom you spend time with.

Pull out your smartphone and flip through your contacts. Think about the people in there. Sooner or later, you'll find someone who doesn't swim in the shallow end. You'll see someone who cares about you beyond your usefulness (and if there's no one like that anywhere in your contacts, it may be time to update the list). For the men who would go a step further with you, could it be time for you to spend more energy seeking their company?

Adam went through a stretch where business didn't go well. "In recent years, I spent a significant amount of time trying to nurse it back to health, but I got to the end of my rope. Then, during a meeting with my mastermind group, they asked me, 'Have you reached out to anyone in your network for help with this?'"

Adam was busted, caught failing to follow his own advice. "After that, everything recovered quickly," he said. "I had forgotten how everything I've ever accomplished can be traced to knowing and building quality connections with the right people."

So, does it take hard work and a lot of time to build a quality relationship with someone? Doesn't it depend a lot on the other person being equally interested and committed? Well, in a word, yes. And also, no.

It's true—no matter how kind, generous and uplifting you might be toward them—some people just won't reciprocate. They may not be malicious, mean-spirited, obnoxious or self-centered. They simply lack the maturity to appreciate such things.

It's like trying to get my dog—a good friend if ever there was one—to show appreciation when I arrange for someone to feed and walk him while I'm away. He'll gladly accept the food and exercise without wondering or caring how it happened. He'll never get curious about why I did it or send me a thank-you note. When I return, he'll be up for the next game of fetch and enjoy my company all the same. He's a great buddy, but he's also a dog. My thoughtfulness is simply not a category he considers.

No, I'm not saying most people are dogs, but they can operate like dogs when it comes to friendship! If you want to improve your community, you need to become a giver. You need to find a community full of givers. And then, you need to give to them and stop wasting time with the dogs.

Luch agreed: What we do for each other, we do for God. It makes sense. You can't see God or touch Him, and few people have stories of Him speaking audibly. But you can do all three of those things with other people who are also His children whom He loves. I've heard people talk about "verticals and horizontals," when it comes to this. What you do with God is "vertical," but what you do for others is "horizontal." Could our isolation stem from needing more "horizontals" in our lives?

"When you show up, God shows up," said Luch. "He tells us to love, honor and encourage one another. So if we're people full of F.A.I.T.H.—Faithful, Available, Initiators who are Teachable and have a Heart for God—we can take the lead and invite people into a community. And they don't even have to be committed believers if you're adaptable."

Steph invited a friend named James into the Mavericks group. Soon, James confided in Steph about difficulties he faced. "James already knew of my involvement in the Mavericks," Steph said. "He was a little apprehensive because he thought it was a 'religious group.' But after that initial visit, he felt more comfortable. I began to invite him to our retreats and events, and he came! Once he'd experienced it, he stayed. He kept meeting new people and became part of the community."

This sounded better than what passes for "evangelism" these days. A group of guys welcomed a guy who wanted nothing to do with religion, they disarmed him with sincerity and love, and he came home to God! Maybe that's how we're meant to convert people.

Here's another thrive inhibitor: We short-sell our failures, struggles and folly when we refuse to be vulnerable.

"We're all broken individuals, and we don't want anyone to know," said Dean. "We tend to forget . . . either we're going through things or we've gone through things. But we think we're the only ones. Then, as soon as we tell the truth, we realize that we're among friends. We're surrounded by people who thought they were the only ones."

Could your failures be valuable if they give hope to others? Better yet, isn't it remarkable how goodness can come even from things you thought you had to keep hidden forever?

At rock bottom, Warren Peterson went to a conference he couldn't afford to attend to hear a message he couldn't afford to miss. He learned to be honest about things he thought he couldn't afford to share. "I'd probably be dead if I hadn't gone to that conference," he said. "On the way home, I cried out to God with everything in me and gave it all to Him."

Stripped of his fierce independence and isolation, Warren discovered his true mission: To bring together like-minded warriors seeking a tribe and a game plan for a beyond-average life. He evolved as a faith-filled business-man. Significant Man gathers men through intensive train-ing events and then walks through life with them through the mastermind experience.

What does it look like to thrive in brotherhood?

Adam offered perspective about how to think when build-ing a network: "First, it's a numbers game," he said. "If you can find a group of five excellent men, you're 'the sixth.'" But remember: There aren't just five other people. By joining, you start to gain access to their networks and the incredible people they know. One introduction leads to another.

"Relational thriving also leads to a surge in confidence. Do you want to be a marketable employee? Attract a spouse? Improve at carrying conversations and persuading people to work with you? Learn to build quality relation-ships. Learn to ask the kind of questions that 'hook' people, get them talking, and keep them coming back for more."

With fatherly wisdom, Luch shared the story of watch-ing a *National Geographic* video with his grandson about a wounded lion encircled by a pack of hyenas. "I told him, 'Watch. These hyenas are going to tear this lion to shreds.' But then, another lion showed up. Now it's TWO lions! And you can imagine who won the battle. I turned to my grandson and said, 'Here's the lesson: make sure you're not the only lion among a group of hyenas!'

"This is about way more than Bible studies," Luch continued. "This is where 'The Word' becomes flesh. Scripture is the resource and fuel for the conversation. But we're after it more for what it does than what it is. If you can show men that this is 'where the metal hits the meat,' that it's about one life connecting with another . . . you're onto something."

Steph added that sharing every part of life, especially losses, make a man more approachable and relatable. "Instead of the old church 'hello' thing, keeping things surface level and never getting deep, you have the opportunity to bare your soul and find hope," he said. "And you also get people's wheels turning. Having an older man like Luch around to share how he handled things is very helpful. It draws me to him rather than scare me away."

I don't know about you, but I've taken some deep, relaxing breaths after finding space to expose issues I thought nobody wanted to know. Aren't you tired of hiding your mess? Wouldn't life feel less painful and overwhelming if you knew you weren't "the only one"?

"Men need to have the type of friendships they can call when their life is falling apart," added Warren. "When a brotherhood is formed, you have someone to walk through life with you. They know your strengths, weaknesses, and goals. They also have the ability to point out your blind spots and help prevent you from doing something you shouldn't."

Is thriving in brotherhood worth it?

A vision paints a picture of a preferred future. Have you thought about what you'd like your life to look like when it comes to friendship and community? Do you think it's possible to visualize a life enriched by fellowship, intimacy, laughter, shared struggle and shared victory? Here are some basics to remember when you begin your journey:

You may not know what will come from seeking brotherhood, but you can trust that it will be good if you build authentic connections.

You may not know how it will turn out, but if you do it with sincerity and gratitude, you can expect better results than if you did nothing.

You may not know who will participate, but if you start with one group of amazing people, it won't be long before you meet more amazing people.

You may not know when or where it will happen, it might happen incrementally over several years. It usually takes time. But then one day, you'll wake up and see how far you've come. And even if it's quite removed from your expectations, it will be good.

You may not know why it works. That's totally fine; you don't need to. You just have to remember that it does work, if you keep at it. True friendships are like dating. Rejection will happen, but if you persist and learn to ask deeper questions at the right time, you'll eventually discover deep-seated connections.

If you find yourself stymied with a lot of things you want to do with your life, it could be time to rethink the frustration as a gift. You're actually receiving real-time results to show you how life "in the shallows" really feels.

You need the type of people you can call when life falls apart. When you have a brotherhood, you have people to walk through life with you. They know your strengths, weaknesses, and goals. They also have the ability to point out your blind spots and help prevent you from doing something you shouldn't.

And don't forget: Community and friendship isn't always about struggles and failures. You also need a safe place to share victories. Wins come and go, and the world is full of people who will either not care or become envious of you. So, share them with your brothers.

One way or another, we all need a tribe.

Reminder: This book was designed to help you in the areas you need it most. If you're reading straight through, great! Keep going. If you're reading this chapter because you took the assessment and now want to jump to the last chapter instead of tackling other Core Areas, go ahead!

You can find additional resources for relationships by listening to the Made to Thrive *podcast episodes featuring these men, or by visiting amithriving.com*

Chapter Five:

HEALTH

God made us to feel good, and to have energy,
a good sex life—and if we're not having
those things, then something in our health
isn't clicking like it should.
— Kevin Davis

We want the life, but not the lifestyle.
— John Mark Comer

My friend Zach Lush used to play professional baseball for the Florida Marlins. Now, he has a growing business partnership, coaching pro athletes on their mental fitness. He'll ask, "If baseball is ninety percent mental, why do we spend most of our time practicing the ten percent physical aspect of the game?"

Forget baseball. Take any sport, from beginner to Olympic levels, and competitive athletes will tell you: The slight edge that gives them victory has nothing to do with genetics, biology, or physical raw material. The winning edge with health and fitness can always be found in the heart, mind, and soul of the athlete.

But we don't read that in fitness magazines driven by advertising revenue. They push supplements and gear to cover their bills. The multi-billion-dollar fitness industry typically under delivers on its promises. They focus on the physical façade, short-changing the customer from the start.

You can't blame the industry entirely. Fitness consumers bring their own list of unrealistic and misguided expectations to the table. The overwhelming majority of adults who start diets and training programs want to lose weight and look good. That's a perfectly fine objective—unless it fails to solve the problem.

Don't get me wrong, you can want weight loss and trim appearance. There's nothing like looking in the mirror and seeing youth, muscle and vigor. It's just that there are more forces aligned against our health than junk food, alcohol, and laziness. We aren't overweight and out of shape by accident or purely because of external substances. Health has more to do with outside appearance than we feel comfortable admitting.

The men in this chapter deal with health and fitness as a mental game where it really counts. They help clients transform by digging into their stories and backgrounds. They know how our bodies move, process substances (like food) and carry ordinary workloads, such as walking or sitting. On the other hand, too many fitness trainers and dieticians treat the symptoms rather than the disease. Plus, most of their customers would prefer to "sprint" (i.e., take a pill or buy magical workout equipment) rather than treat health like a marathon.

Should we expect to thrive in our health if we only want instant, short-term results? That's like using a Band-Aid to stop internal bleeding. We have got to find a better way.

Why aren't men thriving in their health? What's holding them back?

The most difficult person to see clearly is yourself. Have you noticed how obvious it is when your wife, kids, or friends have gifts and talents? You see their uniqueness and appreciate their abilities. But shine that same spotlight on yourself, and the tone suddenly changes. Now, you feel tempted to analyze and diminish your zone of genius.

We don't always see how our pride can "talk us out" of helping ourselves by making changes. We think we have to overcome incredible obstacles, and we don't want the responsibility. Our social circles, meanwhile, are negligent (at best) when it comes to health. We have no one holding us accountable—and we'd like to keep it that way.

This area is the toughest challenge for me, personally. I'm naturally slender with low body fat. You might look at me and say, "What do you have to worry about?" But as you'll read, being skinny with low body fat is just the tip of the iceberg.

When weren't you thriving in health?

I've weighed the same since I graduated from high school. I don't work out, and I eat whatever I want. Sounds like I'm living the dream, right? Not quite. Maintaining a certain scale weight has very little to do with actual health. The fact that my health issues are less visible than some others only makes it more of a threat. I needed these guys to raise my level of consciousness about health and give me practical steps to move forward.

Curtis Hunnicutt

Curtis believes men neglect their health because of a lack of desire. They try to force themselves to adopt a lifestyle they dislike, leaving them in a zero-sum game. You won't last if you think you have to wait forty years before you can ever eat pizza again. "A guy I admire named Ross Edgley has a book about fitness," Curtis said. "It has a pyramid for diet and nutrition. And he argues that the basis for any diet is flavor! If you can't enjoy something, you're eventually going to give up on it."

Who can argue with that? How many people do you know who faithfully persist in doing things they hate? It's sort of like having surgery just because "you have the will to power through it." I'd rather not have the surgery in the first place.

The only good reason for someone to follow a diet they hate is this: You have a life-threatening disease the diet can overcome. Don't ignore obvious medical exceptions that could save your life.

Curtis observed a similar contradiction with exercise and training programs: The fitness industry tries to get people to conform to "one-size-fits-all" programs, and most customers don't like them.

"If you just want to feel good overall, and you find a workout system that serves that purpose, what's wrong with that?" he asked. "Now, if you want to build a bunch of muscle or get really strong, well, then, there are ways to do that too. I just want to figure out what I enjoy doing and go and do that."

In his own journey, Curtis faced inherent physical disadvantages. Standing just five feet four inches tall, he faced many larger opponents in sports. He didn't personally believe he could become stronger or faster. He struggled with proper athletic form, mobility and frequent injuries for most of his life. But thriving wasn't on the radar because Curtis believed that being small, slow, weak and vulnerable were his "lot in life."

Kevin Davis

Kevin recently sold a holistic health practice in Hindman, Kentucky that he owned and operated for many years. He's a physician's assistant and wrote a book with the quintessential refrain of someone who wants to transform their health: *Just Tell Me What To Do*.

"For me, thriving in health is not much of a 'physical' decision," Kevin said. "I certainly enjoy being in good health, but that isn't the core reason. Your health needs to be attached to something much greater if you're going to summon the long-term strength to take ownership of it. I began to think of it in terms of legacy—the kind of example I wanted my children to follow."

As we spoke, Kevin's stories and responses lined up with his emphasis on mindset. "I remember going for a run after a period of not exercising, and getting totally winded in under one mile. That was the dealbreaker for me. I'd never been gassed that quickly from running."

Kevin also emphasizes the company we keep when it comes to fitness. "Another reason I failed in fitness was who spoke into my life at that time," he said. "You have to find a tribe, a group of guys who are on the same mission as you, and lock shields with them if you want to win this game."

Jim Gromer

Jim's journey took a turn for the worse during a trip to Italy as he shot a documentary. Busyness and constant travel kept him from paying attention to his condition.

"I woke up one night with chest pains," he said. "I felt like my heart was burning. I went to the emergency room. Fortunately, I wasn't having heart issues. But this was the wake-up call for me, that something had to change. The heavier you get, the more it affects other parts of your body, like your knees. I didn't want to 'eat' myself out of being able-bodied. I wanted to be around for graduations and weddings."

Sometimes, a trip to the emergency room gets men to take life seriously. Thriving in health is a journey we have to go on, not a switch we can flip. It's also an individual journey. As with golf, your real opponent isn't the other players, it's the course and how you relate to it uniquely as a person.

"We think we have to go on some super-intense program of training like a beast while eating nuts and berries," Jim said, "and that isn't true. Not for the average person, anyway. We tell people to enjoy foods they like in moderation and to use what they already do as a way to exercise."

Cameron Hall

Cam grew up athletic. Tall, muscular and competitive, he became known as "Cam the Fit Guy" in his twenties playing collegiate sports. But life caught up with him in his early thirties as marriage and children took center stage. And his health suffered. "For a long time, I struggled with the 'all-or-nothing' mentality," he said. "It isn't popular to put your health first." If fitness couldn't be front-and-center, Cam didn't see the point of focusing on it.

He also pinpointed "information overload" as a problem. "Most men have no idea what to do or the steps to take," he said. "It's awkward, especially if you're a busy husband and father with a career or business, to find a program that works with your lifestyle. Google and social media bombard us with content and information that may or may not be helpful."

Cam tried to fix his health as a lone wolf using information he'd already learned as a younger man. But what had worked so well in his twenties no longer helped as he took on marriage, children, post-graduate education and full-time work all at the same time. During one stretch, he gained thirty pounds of fat.

Jimmy Page

Growing up in the fitness industry, Jimmy knew what it means to fail in health even while you appear to "succeed." His health began to deteriorate in the middle of building an empire of gyms designed to help others improve theirs. "When my kids were young, we were super-busy," he said. "We worked long hours operating health clubs. I ran from one club to another and one sports field to another as my kids grew up . . . and got into eating junk food. It wasn't long before I was fifteen pounds overweight. One night, I heard God say, 'You lack integrity.'"

Jimmy attributes men's failure to thrive to the "usual suspects" in our heads. We don't think it matters. Nobody teaches us the deep connection between our spiritual and physical lives. We can't see how our bodies and souls communicate with each other.

We men also gravitate toward areas where we find success and avoid areas where we struggle. And over time, Jimmy began to lose heart. With health, the older you get, the less margin you have to make mistakes or recede into old habits without the added consequences of a sense of failure.

How can you go from failure to thriving in health?

After a laundry list of injuries and setbacks, Curtis' health struggle received an unexpected boost. By becoming an entrepreneur, he discovered a much greater purpose in reading and began to devour books about the physical body. "I never set out to create a 'health coaching company,'" he said, "but by working out with friends and practicing accountability, people began to insist on paying me for what I knew." Today, in addition to health coaching, he develops leaders in a network of churches in southern Maryland.

"I realized I had the ability to change my body," he said. "I'd always believed that 'you get what you get' at birth. But reading books like *Think And Grow Rich*, *The Richest Man In Babylon* and *The Compound Effect* shifted my perspective. I started studying things like cold exposure, contrast showers, deep belly breathing and mobility stretching. I got Platelet-rich Plasma (PRP) injections to avoid surgery, and my shoulder healed."

Curtis also emphasized his commitment to a "trial-and-error" approach with diets and training to thrive in health:

"You become a guinea pig everywhere," he said. "You try different styles, read different books, go to different places. When your health journey is based on experimentation, you'll find depth wherever you apply your mind. I like working with old people for that very reason—they're willing to try a lot of different things."

Curtis also mentioned a major theme of thriving in all seven areas—accountability. But here's the caveat: Accountability will not work if you don't have a sense of purpose behind it.

"With my coaching clients, we do it together through challenges," he explained. "Sometimes, people aren't clear on 'why' they seek change. One struggled to work on himself until his first child was born, but afterward, it was much easier to be accountable. In my case, it was after I gave my life to Christ in 2015. Fitness stopped being about my reputation and became about self-improvement and the ability to enjoy life."

Kevin agreed. "It comes back to who's on your right and left. When that bench has the right people on it, you'll be amazed."

And then there's the science. Kevin used the phrase "fat-adapted" to describe thriving in health. "You can burn sugar, or you can burn fat, but you can't do both," he said. Kevin encourages people to let him look underneath the hood, such as blood work and urinalysis, to better understand their bodies' unique chemistries.

That makes sense. I eat the same as many of my friends who weigh 50-100 pounds more than I do, but I don't gain weight. Our bodies' chemistry must be unique, like our personalities.

Jim also provided some data-driven reasons for thriving in health. He cited a fascinating study from a few years back assessing the health of people at every fitness level. It ran the gamut—from people with life-threatening medical conditions to Olympic athletes (who, funnily enough, are also knocking on heaven's door because of how athleticism taxes their bodies).

"The bottom twenty percent of people pay absolutely zero attention to their health," said Jim, "and the best news is that doing something— anything—reduces your risk of death from health-related complications by as much as fifty-five percent." Walk for twenty minutes a day, run for ten, and you get the same benefit to your health? Did you understand that? It means we can relax, and we don't need steroids, or twigs and berries. In fact, according to Jim, we can even enjoy a donut or a beer now and again.

What does it look like to thrive in health?

"Our prescription for thriving in physical health is what we call 'The M.E.R.C.Y. Rule,'" Jim said. "The 'M' stands for **movement**, and it means you have to do something physically active throughout your day. Walk, run, bike, skate, or lift. Do something to break the sedentary lifestyle. 'Sitting' is the new 'smoking.'

"The 'E' stands for **eat** smarter. We tell people to replace at least three bad choices with three healthy choices each day. Don't bother with traditional dieting; you'll most likely end up putting the weight back on.

"The 'R' is for **rest**, which means we have to get off of sugar, caffeine and to stop acting as our own pharmacists. A big reason we overeat is because we're dehydrated, and we're dehydrated because we consume too many stimulants.

"The 'C' stands for **connect**, which means that the best way to improve your health is, you guessed it, in community with a loved one or friend.

"And the 'Y' stands for **you**. No one else, including God, is going to make this change for you. You're the only one with the power to choose it."

This opened my eyes. Nowhere in any of these conversations did these men tell me I had to run 100 miles a day, bench press a metric ton or contort myself like a pretzel. For the first time, thriving in health and fitness felt possible.

On an invitation from his wife, Cam went to a health conference and found himself exposed to new guidance on how to use food as fuel instead of trying to survive without eating: "I discovered that true health goes way beyond aesthetics," he said. "Those difficult seasons of gaining weight didn't just affect my body. They affected my identity and career. They damaged my confidence, especially when I was actually able to lose some of the weight, only to gain it back."

Some time later, a friend teased Cam about "giving in to the dad bod." Indignantly, he replied, "F the dad bod." It became a running joke. However, one day, Cam decided to use the phrase to start a new business called Fight The Dad Bod. For three years now, he's helped hundreds of fathers shed belly fat and get in the best shape of their lives.

"Fitness is about living healthy for yourself and your family," Cam said. "A lot of dads ignore the signs of failing health, the same way I did. But it doesn't have to be that way. You can do more than fight extra pounds. You can learn about how food works with your body and find a science-based program you can stick with for the rest of your life."

Hearing God tell him, "You lack integrity," caused Jimmy to reach his boiling point. "I called a family meeting," he said. "I threw out every last ounce of that junk food and told them, 'We're never eating fast food again.'"

This turning point fundamentally altered their path. The Page family transformed the way they ate and made it into a lifestyle. "It's a culture of health," Jimmy said. "We identify ourselves quite clearly as 'different' from the majority. Over time, we learned to create mantras and statements around this, such as 'I train every day.' We would put fitness events like 5K runs, or Spartan races on a future date, and challenge ourselves to train for them."

Jimmy eventually wrote a book with two other authors called *One Word*. It guides readers on a journey of making an entire resolution under a single word discerned through prayer and reflection.

"My friends and I would get together to set New Year's Resolutions, but they never worked," he explained. "After a couple of weeks, we'd forget all about them. Then somebody suggested we make a resolution around a single word and see what God would do with it. That was when we began to see tremendous change. Instead of life being all about what we could accomplish, it was now about whom we would become."

What if our physical bodies are powerful statements about who we are and who we're becoming? What if they aren't just utilitarian vehicles, but instead unique, tangible expressions of the spiritual being inside?

"Keep trying new things," said Curtis. "There's never just one way to do something. For each person, there's something unique that we can enjoy and respond to. A habit is something that's hard not to do. Each person's success looks different, so why should you try to do the same things I do?"

Is thriving in health worth it?

Curtis continued, "Satan wants us to believe that when we fail, we have to go all the way back to square one. But the truth is that you've fallen where you've fallen. The only thing that matters is whether or not you get back up." Challenges and difficulties go with the territory of being human, but we keep trying to find a shortcut! If you learned to see setbacks as normal, could you 'hang in there' more often?

Kevin believes we always retain some degree of authority over our genetic structure. "There's genetics," he said, "and then there are epigenetics. Our lifestyle has the ability to activate (or deactivate) how our genes respond." That gave me something to think about. "Genetics" feels inevitable, like your eye color. Only it's not—not totally, anyway.

Genetics go way beyond your individual molecular makeup. Kevin paints it in the category of altering your family tree. Most people think of "money" when they hear the term legacy, but Kevin describes it as "the lifestyle and path" we can offer our kids through consistent habits and behavior. Could it be, with everything we've learned about the interconnectedness of our being, that we can somehow "speak" to our genetics? Meanwhile, our kids get daily exposure to how we eat, exercise, rest and treat our own bodies for the first eighteen years of their lives. Shouldn't you set an example worth following?

Let's say you hopped a plane from Denver, where I live, to Washington D.C. If the pilots or navigation system get even one degree off from where they're supposed to be, chances are you'd end up in Baltimore. Jim argues the same in reverse: If you change just one thing from how you currently steward your health, you'll end up in an entirely better place. If you go from sitting for eight hours to sitting for seven hours and forty minutes (and walk the other twenty), you'll improve.

Of course, once you build a habit of walking twenty minutes a day, you can start shooting for thirty, forty, or sixty minutes a day. Success has a way of breeding more success. Once you feel "better," you'll want to start feeling "better-er."

"It's never too late to take control of your health," added Cam. "Right now is the starting point, but that doesn't mean it's where you'll finish. We coach people on their overall health, including the mental side—because without your health, you have nothing."

This also has nothing to do with surgery, magic pills and fad diets. "It's good old sleep, nutrition, exercise, water, and vitamins and minerals," said Cam. "The same way you'd be concerned about what your kids eat. There's nothing to be afraid of and no great mystery. You can do this."

Jimmy added, "Invest in your wellness now, or you'll pay for your illness later. You don't know how 'bad' you actually feel until you feel better. Once you start an exercise routine, you'll feel optimistic. You'll sleep better. Your energy will improve, and it'll have a positive 'ripple effect' on everything else."

We can do this. It is possible. Of all the things within our control in life, make health chief among them. You won't find it easy or satisfying in the beginning stages, but everyone who's ever done it tells me the same thing: Once you get the momentum going, it snowballs and breeds more success.

So, let's not wait any longer.

Reminder: This book was designed to help you in the areas you need it most. If you're reading straight through, great! Keep going. If you're reading this chapter because you took the assessment and now want to jump to the last chapter instead of tackling other Core Areas, go ahead!

You can find additional resources for health by listening to the Made to Thrive *podcast episodes featuring these men, or by visiting amithriving.com*

Chapter Six:

FINANCES

Compound interest is the eighth wonder
of the world. He who understands it, earns it;
he who doesn't, pays it.
— **Albert Einstein**

If then you have not been faithful in the unrighteous
wealth, who will entrust to you the true riches?
— **Luke 16:11**

We attach an awful lot of labels and descriptions to money. What words or phrases come to mind when you think about it?

The halls of academia, for the most part, fail to teach financial literacy. You'd expect it from institutions that teach mathematics from kindergarten to university and churn out people who can add, subtract, multiply and divide. If only money was as simple as math.

The average person doesn't understand money, for the most part. People do strange things with it across a broad spectrum. Some people get into debt so deep that they apply for another credit card to try to get out of it. Others hoard and save so much that they hide large quantities of cash among their foodstuffs in case of emergency. They "step over dollars to pick up dimes," as the saying goes. Now multiply this by millions of people, and you get an imbalance in the value of our currency.

Most men live somewhere in the middle of those two extremes. But most men do not thrive financially. This piqued my curiosity. In a society that routinely accuses us of out-earning women by thirty percent, how can so many of us be hurting for cash?

More importantly—is money good, evil, both or neither? What makes a piece of paper with certain colors and inscriptions on it "valuable" anyway? Why is there so much confusion and variance in the value of a dollar versus any other value of measurement?

In gathering wisdom on this subject, I came to the conclusion that the papers, coins and plastic cards we think of as "money" are mere representations. But what do they represent? How do we actually know a dollar's worth?

I assembled financial professionals for this chapter. They spend their time and energy educating people about financial decisions. I wanted to hear how they handle this subject so fraught with emotional reactions, from one man to the next.

Within that emotional component lies the secret. Money is dynamic because, in reality, it is not a mere number You see, money expresses value—the individual's unique sense of what they value and how much they value it. This might help explain the saying, "One man's trash is another man's treasure."

I discovered again: Money isn't the problem. We are. Out of every creature on this planet, only we use it. Plus, only we mishandle it. But not everyone handles money the same way. Some people steward it wisely, creating generational wealth for their children's children. Others squander every penny they get their hands on. Most of us do "okay" with it. We could thrive, but we don't.

Let's put it this way: Have you ever stopped to ask yourself what you'd really do if you suddenly inherited a fortune? Do you know yourself well enough to predict how you'd respond, or would you merely blurt out a laundry list of things you'd like to buy, the way little kids do?

Understanding why you feel fear, anxiety, greed, contempt or recklessness with money will help you change directions. We can't overcome our barriers to freedom unless we define them. So, let's dive in and learn the truth about thriving financially.

Why aren't men thriving in their finances? What's holding them back?

We can physically count our money, but it rarely behaves in a linear, mathematical, add-and-subtract fashion. Have you ever lived paycheck-to-paycheck, as many Americans do? Apart from their spending habits, why is every dollar already spoken for by the time they get paid? Don't answer; just sit with the question.

Conversely, why do Americans like Warren Buffett earn more money without working, soaking up pennies with every breath they take? Again, don't answer; just sit with the question.

Why does money top the list of contention points between husbands and wives? How come it drives so many divorces? Clearly, the problem runs way deeper than addition and subtraction.

And why can't we just get simple truth and guidance? There's a biased culture among professionals. Unbiased, unhurried guidance is rare in a culture that prizes sales and uses so much jargon.

Automation and convenience block men from thriving. Financial success seems like too much work. Can't we just push a button or pull a lever to gain financial independence? Why all this strategic thinking? There should be an app for this.

Men frequently postpone seeking help until their thirties or forties because just getting started feels incredibly complicated. In our early twenties, we say, "I'll worry about that later." But we pay for it when we reach our forties and wish we'd put in the work earlier.

This one really stuck out: The more discretionary income a man has, the likelier he is to use it to build a *lifestyle* rather than a life. Did you catch that? A lifestyle versus a life. There is a difference, and the choices a man makes when he has the privilege and responsibility of stewarding resources say a lot about his heart and character.

Some guys are wise to the trick and think of nobler things: Paying off debt, saving for college and weddings, helping struggling family members or donating to causes they care about. Do you have a list of problems, whether they affect you directly or not, that you would solve if you had the money?

When weren't you thriving in finances?

Out of the 7 Core Areas, finances are the worst barometer for whether you're thriving in life. We all know people who have plenty of money, but fail to thrive in all the other areas. However, finances are the easiest one of these areas to measure. We have to carefully separate the baby and the bathwater here.

David Littlejohn

A background in journalism gave David the curiosity he brings to advising clients. "I've learned to approach the process with a million questions," he said. "I'm obsessed with understanding why people think and behave the ways they do with money."

With more than two decades advising families and businesses in the small town of Roseburg, Oregon, David believes men lack this curiosity. "Men bring a lot of baggage into their financial decisions," he told me. "Most of the time, they're unaware of how they're either rebelling against (or complying with) their parents' ways of dealing with money."

Ouch. Do you mean to tell me that more than twenty years after I moved out, the ways Mom and Dad handled money still influence the way I handle it? Well, maybe. David says it could also come from a lack of understanding others—particularly, "others" who work in advertising and marketing. Do you take what you hear from culture, advertising, marketing, and the media at face value? Or with a grain of salt?

"Most people don't understand how the system works," David said. "They get their financial education from advertising, which is a horrible source for it. They don't understand the difference between 'needs' and 'wants.' It's tough to make sound decisions with terrible habits and lousy information."

Okay. I feel a little better. Maybe it isn't Mom and Dad. It's more like being a quarterback who refuses to exercise, playing for the Cleveland Browns. Sure, you wear the uniform and the logos, but that's it.

Lance Belline

Affable and down-to-earth, Lance Belline built a strong team of advisers, accountants, and staff at his firm, Lighthouse Financial, in Rogers, Arkansas. Lance believes men struggle with money because of poor communication from the industry. Advisers operate in silos and it leads to miscommunication. "We keep to ourselves and don't share information," he said. "But when we do that, it's the client that pays a steep price. We lose out on truly satisfying them, and the only real 'winner' is the IRS. Something's wrong with that picture."

Lance grew weary of the "pain management" approach to advising clients. They would consult with him, hoping to grow and keep more of their money in retirement—only to pay a fortune in taxes anyway.

It may not surprise you to hear this: Pride is back again, preventing men from thriving with finances. Lance noticed through years of attempting to educate people about money. "Guys don't want to look like fools," Lance said, "so they sit there and nod their heads as the adviser talks through the plan. But in reality, they have no idea what's being conveyed. Or they simply don't want help with finances."

I can imagine that one. Men feel the burden of social expectation as traditional breadwinners. They know they receive strict judgment for their performance, so they try to window-dress it and make it look like they know what they're doing. It works well, until it doesn't.

Adam Carroll

As the founder of Mastery of Money, Adam Carroll educates thousands of people about financial transformation. He cites poor emotional health and stunted literacy as core reasons for men's financial failures. He also added an interesting twist:

"I'm a contrarian personality," he said. "So when I choose an adviser, I tend to look for someone with a similar temperament, in addition to shared values and objectives. I want someone who is already thriving, of course. But I also want them to challenge my assumptions and ideas. I don't want a 'yes-man,' even one with a solid character and good strategy."

Now we're talking. We fail to seek advisers who don't shy from telling us we're wrong. We try to hide our incompetence, afraid of how we'll look when we don't know everything. Guys who get over their own pride have everything to gain. Do you have enough self-awareness to have strong convictions that you can still hold loosely? Are you willing to go against your own instincts or experience if someone presents a compelling alternative?

Try this: Take a look at the men around you. If you judge on behavior, most men fail to thrive financially because the answer to these questions is, "No." Most men don't want to be challenged because relaxing their convictions or admitting they don't have answers feels like an anathema to proper manhood. It isn't taught, modeled or preached; it's not "the manly way."

Clark Bradley

Together with his wife, Clark Bradley seized the events of 2020 to start a company called "Igniting Financial Freedom." But up until then, the Bradleys served as poster children for the 'American Financial Nightmare'—debt, poor spending/saving habits, conflict, and anxiety. And Clark couldn't figure out why.

"I was preoccupied with the noise of the world," Clark said. "I think we go down the 'lazy river' without much conviction. There's so much noise, distraction, and numbness at our fingertips. It's easy to be comfortable and complacent— you think, 'I have a family, a house, kids. I checked the boxes, and I'm good.'"

Do you tick the same boxes Clark does? Are you comfortable and complacent, buried under a mountain of debt? That house you "own," does it belong to you or to the bank that lent you the money? Do you struggle to deal with unforeseen price tags due to a lack of planning?

Brad Barrett

We know we're in trouble if certified public accountants (CPAs) are financially illiterate, and Brad Barrett was. "I'd never taken classes on personal finance," he said. "As a society, we don't know anything about it. We sweep it under the rug, avoiding discussion or attempts to understand the details. We put the blame on the anonymous 'they.'"

I liked the idea of the anonymous "they." Do you have any idea how often I make excuses and blame it on someone called "they"? Clearly, "they" also play a role in my writer's block.

"The biggest stressor in our lives is finances," Brad continued. "We've all made catastrophic mistakes with them. In my twenties, I was a CPA and I 'should' have known better. Instead, I went and got suckered because I didn't know what to do with my money. I lost a lot of sleep throughout that decade and didn't reach financial independence until I was forty."

How can you go from failure to thriving in finances?

Men could do with better explanations of value. "We're less conscious of the value we give when we earn money than we are of the value we obtain when we spend it," David pointed out. "If you don't think of yourself as 'worth' earning more, you're going to struggle."

Isn't that the truth? I've played enough sports to know that if I pre-determine I will lose, something amazing happens: I lose! The same goes for money. It won't flow to you if you think of yourself as a loser who doesn't deserve it. Plus, is it really a good idea to walk around believing you aren't worth your salt?

A lot of what we'd call "thriving" with finances sounds like overkill if you live in the "basement" of Maslow's hierarchy of needs. If you only expect to earn a mediocre wage to meet your basic physical needs, don't expect to thrive.

But remember, if you say, "No" to income growth and prosperity, you say, "Yes" to problems money can solve. Do you find so much virtue in poverty that you'd pass up the resources to impact people's lives for the better? Should you complain about the costs of living if you refuse to grow and get better?

Lance allied himself with a five-member "study group" of financial planners in different cities, spread far apart. "With multiple minds that aren't competing with each other, you discover angles and ways of looking at things you can't see by yourself," he said. "A man in my study group presented a series of questions during a meeting. Under my breath, I dismissed each one—until he explained them. Suddenly, it clicked. I was sitting on a goldmine and didn't know it."

Lance began to apply strategy to everything. He partnered with a CPA, so his firm could consult on both ends of financial decisions. Together, they'd recommend a roadmap to build wealth and pay fewer taxes. And clients' portfolios did exactly what Lance thought—they grew. More importantly, they stayed large and plentiful well into the clients' retirement years. "I'd been serving people sincerely, but incorrectly, for years," said Lance. "There's a difference, it turns out, between doing 'good things' and getting 'optimal results.'"

Adam had a brilliant way of thinking about finances: "Most people's financial journey sounds like this: They go to work, they get paid, they go to work, they get paid, repeat. I didn't want to do that forever. I wanted to work, then get paid—and then get paid, get paid again and get paid some more. I wanted to earn in one day what I normally earned in a month."

Could we be passing up extra money by hanging onto the nine-to-five, trusting in a combination of Social Security and 401(k)s to get us through the end stages of life? Could it be mindset and positioning that keep us from thriving?

Adam asks two excellent questions about finances:

1. "What would it require for you to earn in one day, or one hour, what most people earn in a month or a year?"
2. "How do you pay the least amount of taxes and interest on debt?"

Those questions will nudge you in the right direction. They remind me of something Tony Robbins said: "The more you ask yourself good questions, the more good answers you get in return."

Clark's story took a few curves. He and his wife Jennifer got married in 2010 under financial stress—both of them carried college debt, and they took on new debts to home improvement and consumer credit card lenders—to the tune of $95,000.

By the middle of the decade, the Bradleys were fed up. They went through Dave Ramsey's *Financial Peace* course and brought their debt down to a much more manageable $12,000. But as Clark confessed, they hadn't fully learned their lesson. They went out and purchased a second home, replacing nearly every dollar of debt they'd wiped out.

At rock bottom in 2016, Clark realized it boiled down to a failure to honor his own commitments. "You can write your goals, and then a month goes by, and you don't honor what you write," he said. "My mindset had shifted, but I was still overspending. While working as a financial coach at a bank! I was there to help clients manage their money, yet I was hauling bags of aluminum cans to the recycling center at nighttime to pay my electric bill!"

What does it look like to thrive in finances?

"Money is a tool," said David, "and the more you see it as just that—a tool—the more you thrive." I've also heard money spoken of as an "amplifier" of the person who possesses it. If you're a jerk when you're broke, you'll be an even bigger jerk when you're rich. If you're a prince when you're penniless, you'll be a good king when you're wealthy.

It turns out, men with the healthiest relationships to money have something in common: Radical honesty. Disclosure is their standard operating procedure. "Is there a conflict?" David asked. "Disclose it. Is there an 'elephant in the room'? Name it. If you're thriving financially, you don't wait for others to create trust. You do it."

Lance's clients are some of the most financially satisfied and generous people on the face of the earth. "They understand how to think strategically with money," he said, "but in a way where the welfare of people they care about is 'baked-in.' They feel like winners who escape the clutches of the taxman. But it isn't about greed. They use the money they avoid paying to the IRS and instead elevate everyone's standard of living, as opposed to just their own."

Lance believes you gain more self-control and mastery when you get this part right. "If you develop a strong sense of stewardship, you can let money flow freely in and out of your life," he said. "You're not as attached to it as people are when they're broke or in debt. You become better at handling life well because it matters much more than your bank balance."

Adam concurred by saying, "There's so much more room for enjoying yourself and the people you love the most. If you're broke, you know how disheartening it is when even simple things go wrong, like your car needing maintenance. But where I live, you don't even blink at a car repair bill. You just pay it and move on with your life."

Brad emphasized the lack of stress. "There are no surprises," he said. "Expenses are on autopilot. When life happens, you're okay! You're not worried about cash flow. And it gets better over time—you vacation and travel more. You enjoy life because your spending reflects your values. You don't try to 'keep up with the Joneses.'"

I like this approach. It's both responsible and fun, as opposed to irresponsible or boring. Sometimes the nerd rules and keeps the free spirit grounded in reality. At other times, the free spirit leads and keeps the nerd from turning into a troll under a bridge.

Is thriving in finances worth it?

Time affects money, both positively and negatively. The more time you have left on planet Earth, the more opportunity you have to thrive. But even if there's less time than there used to be, there's plenty of reason for hope and reason to share lessons learned with younger generations.

As Lao Tzu said, "The journey of a thousand miles begins with a single step." The best part about learning to thrive financially? It operates like compound interest—the result of making a thousand small decisions faithfully. You could think of these decisions as "deposits" that, at some point in the future, enable you to make massive withdrawals without penalties.

Let's be honest: Thriving in finances has a huge positive effect on every other area. Winston Churchill said courage is the most important quality because it guarantees the other ones. We see a loose parallel to that when we consider how money affects the other Core Areas.

Healthy finances can support growth and change in ways that a poor man's existence doesn't allow. Money can complicate your identity. But if we're being honest, most poor men also have terrible senses of identity, don't they? It's much easier to sit with the question, "Who am I?" and wait for an answer when there's no one banging on your door to collect a debt.

Does financial thriving contribute to your mission? Is the Pope Catholic? How much more impact can you make in the lives of others when you don't need to worry where your next paycheck will come from? How many charities and nonprofits do you know that don't bother with fundraising because they have enough?

Is your health easier to maintain with solid finances? You can pay for preventative things like coaching, nutritionists, premium foods and supplements. You can pay more medical bills with money than without it (even as costly as medical care is in some places). Furthermore, you can pay for your kids' care, such as dermatologists or cosmetic dentistry. Can the poor man do such things?

Will thriving with money make you better with faith? Well, why don't you ask Dave Ramsey? If you know how to create wealth, why not teach one of his Financial Peace courses in church? Why not recruit young adults in the church into your business and give them a career path?

Career prospects look better with thriving finances. You can afford additional education, certification, and coaching. You can take (calculated) risks in your career or start a business of your own. Later, you can leverage your skills in a consulting role. Lastly, you can build great relationships when you understand money—everyone's interested in earning more of it.

Does money help relationships? You bet it does. Can you be a better husband with more cash? Are date nights, getaways, sitters and couples-only trips more or less affordable?

Your wife and kids won't remember many of the things you can buy with money, but they'll never forget the experiences of sharing life with you. Why not make those experiences amazing? Why not create them with allies and close friends, and follow through on becoming a true brotherhood?

So, is it worth it? Absolutely. Don't forget, in a financial sense, you have a mission to carry out. You have issues to resolve. The reason you have them in the first place is to overcome them, not to cope indefinitely with stress and awkwardness. We all want to live with intention and purpose. We want the ability to do things we want to do. Thriving financially creates peace, happiness, and contentment where you are.

It's time to aim for *life* rather than lifestyle. It's time to thrive with your finances.

Reminder: This book was designed to help you in the areas you need it most. If you're reading straight through, great! Keep going. If you're reading this chapter because you took the assessment and now want to jump to the last chapter instead of tackling other Core Areas, go ahead!

You can find additional resources for finances by listening to the Made to Thrive *podcast episodes featuring these men, or by visiting amithriving.com*

Chapter Seven:

CAREER

Work to become, not to acquire.
— **Elbert Hubbard**

Let us realize that: the privilege to work
is a gift, the power to work is a blessing,
the love of work is success!
— **David O. McKay**

How do you tackle the one area of a man's life where we see a higher average of "success," but very little thriving? Society and culture encourage men to define ourselves by occupation. In a social setting, we often ask this question first: "What do you do?" This conversation may give us pride or shame—or something in between.

In our age, career and work are being redefined. We're nearly a decade into an experimental era where younger generations are walking away from the traditional "nine-to-five" in droves. Popular books like Tim Ferriss' *The 4-Hour Workweek* and Dan Miller's *48 Days to the Work You Love* encourage people to pursue more than a paycheck from their careers.

I'm actively rolling out a consulting company called Career Factors, based on years of working with unhappy people and reverse engineering career satisfaction. Career Factors identify four other keys to career satisfaction beyond job title and salary. This comes at a time when people are leaving traditional jobs and industries to redefine what work means for them. To find out more, visit the-careerfactors.com.

Major shifts in the industry aren't necessarily bad. The digital revolution has turned many former jobseekers and "wage slaves" into millionaires out of necessity. The "gig economy" offers people paid work from their homes. If you can adjust, this is one of the best times in history to pursue a career. Work can be highly profitable and very convenient.

But even with all this abundance, do most men thrive in their careers? You and I both know the answer to that. Some fail because they're unemployed, lazy, or worse. I'm not here to give them a swift kick and say, "Get to work!" Reading books very seldom solves the problems associated with a broken mindset.

Most men reading this will find themselves gainfully employed. Their work consumes a huge portion of their time, and they may feel quite happy to continue that way. More often than not, they earn money, but don't thrive. They would love to quit and do something they truly enjoy, but fear and responsibility keep them put.

Which would you choose? Both have advantages and drawbacks. If your work is a success, like it was for Femi Doyle-Marshall in Chapter Three, could you close up shop? Could you drop it at a moment's notice if a higher calling emerged?

What about when you can't stand your job? What will it cost you to remain there? Sure, you'll draw a paycheck and keep the bills paid. But does fear of failure or taking risks hold you back? What if you're failing in the other Core Areas because you're settling for "scraps" in this one?

Only one option that answers those questions: Thriving. You feed your family, pay your bills, earn your keep and build for the future, and you draw fulfillment and joy from the process. Thriving means you stop thinking of work as a burdensome chore and see it instead as a privilege and responsibility.

Why aren't men thriving in their career? What's holding them back?

Men face social pressure and enjoy tangible rewards to work hard—a carrot-and-stick routine. As we've covered, plenty of men take their careers to heart and give them weight they should reserve for identity. This leads to a lot of economic activity, but not much thriving.

If you've given your life thus far to the marketplace, you can relax. I'm not about to tell you to renounce work and spend your life in a monastery, peeling onions. You don't have to "sell everything you have, give it to the poor and start over," just to prove you're not a workaholic.

Remember, however, finding success in your career doesn't equate to thriving. If you have to sacrifice the other six areas to achieve success, you're in trouble. The marketplace is littered with men with fragile identities, failed or non-existent relationships, misplaced faith, unanswered missions, poor health, and deep pockets.

When weren't you thriving in career?

This category hit home for me. I left a career in education after twenty-one years. I wanted a greater impact in the world, but I found myself limited by my job title and the expectations placed on me. Maybe you've been in a similar situation, thinking you had 'career' figured out, until a big switch-up happens halfway through. Either way, we can learn a thing or two about thriving in career from these guys.

Anil Ramdin

Anil learned the pitfalls of success as an immigrant with lofty aspirations and heavy cultural expectations. His career took off, and before too long he fell into the same trap. If he succeeded, everyone would approve. Failure, on the other hand, would be catastrophic to his identity.

"We feel we have to meet others' expectations," he said. "So we base our decisions on conventional wisdom, or people's opinions, without a lot of self-awareness. I put a lot of grandiose expectations on earning money and taking care of my family."

This mentality has a "lulling" effect on men. We over-simplify our aspirations into "making money," especially when it actually works. No wonder men think the purpose of making money is to make more money. Anil couldn't help himself. "My career was going great! I spent several years cruising along, thinking, 'I'm fine!' I lived off the satisfaction from meeting others' expectations of what I should do."

Paul Edwards

For other men, Paul's story might hit closer to home. Deeply ambitious and blessed with literary and expressive talent, his career stalled for twenty years because of, wait for it, pride. He wanted to become highly influential in media and writing, but spent his thirties chasing his tail, working as an insurance salesman.

"It was two decades of mediocrity and frustration," he said. "And I trace it all back to a prideful habit of making big, life-changing decisions without seeking advice. I didn't think I needed outside eyes in my life, and I paid a steep price for it. I was constantly unsettled, filled with envy, resentment, bitterness, and sarcasm."

Paul drifted from one job to the next as a young man, quitting or getting fired. Weary of this, he enlisted in the military (where he couldn't quit or get fired). "All that time, I made decisions on a whim," he said. "My main problem was that I preferred to feel rather than think. I would make life-altering decisions in the blink of an eye and then wonder why I reaped the consequences."

A big hurdle for a lot of men is getting them to take life seriously. "I don't mean 'serious' as in 'somber' or 'melancholy,'" Paul clarified. "It's just that we don't want to have to think or consider the magnitude of our decisions. So many things are done for us; we grow up on autopilot. When we make decisions, we don't want to be questioned or have to make a persuasive argument to support what we believe."

Curtis Swisher

Over a thirty-year journey in corporate America, Curtis wrestled to understand the significance of a man's work. Viewed through a lens of faith, he came to know his position as an engineer at Dow Chemical as a platform to be "salt and light" to the world. It helped at the time, but these days, corporate America don't necessarily provide the best environment for exercising faith.

If you have co-workers, you'll soon identify what kind of culture rules your workplace. The old sayings are true: "Misery loves company," and "Bad company corrupts good character." The people you work with can easily influence you in the wrong direction when it comes to your perspective about your career. Sometimes, like in Curtis' case, they can be relatively benign—even legitimate, for a season. But they'll play a huge role in the influence they exert on your identity.

Curtis agreed: "Men fail to thrive in their careers because they're usually in a combination of a wrong external environment and a disempowering internal environment." The day eventually came that Dow no longer found him useful, and there was no room for sentimental loyalty or kindness. They terminated his position.

Scott Beebe

"The number one reason men fail to thrive is chaos," Scott said. "And plenty of people are willing to tell you, 'We're going to liberate you from it.'" I asked what he meant by chaos. He said, "Chaos feels like conflict without resolve," he continued. "In music notes, when a song resolves, it feels good. When it doesn't resolve, you feel discord. It's the same thing internally; when I feel discord in my life, I take it as a metric of not thriving."

Scott's definition of "chaos" is different from how it's usually portrayed—as random events or things that pick us off. Scott believes we intentionally increase chaos in our lives. "We hang onto things and overload our time," he said. "It's what we purposefully take on that destroys us."

Scott founded his company, My Business On Purpose, with the concept of setting "fire" to the ways we cripple ourselves through overload. And here I was, blaming everyone but myself for all the extra things I have to do.

Seth Buechley

Seth tied men's failure with thriving to the proportion of their ambitions. "Ambitious people struggle to find satisfaction," he said, "and satisfied people struggle to find ambition."

When he said that, I felt like he had just shown me top-secret, classified documents leaked from the NSA. "Ambitious men chase things that don't really matter and miss out on things that truly do," he continued. "Everyone else holds on to 100-year-old attitudes about work. They think they're 'here to pay bills for the family and not to find satisfaction.' They have zero vision to thrive."

With a lengthy career in consulting and mergers and acquisitions—and as the author of a book called *Ambition*—Seth should know a thing or two about lofty dreams and ideals. To learn those things, however, means heavy losses. And to rise after falling hundreds of times requires a man to interpret failures differently than how ninety-nine percent of people do.

How can you go from failure to thriving in career?

Like many men, Anil's career went along in cruise control when it got derailed by a significant personal change. For him, it was the birth of a special-needs child. "I looked at that kid and saw the choices I needed to make to be there for him, and the switch flipped," he remembered. "The corporate job just wasn't going to work anymore. So, I started coaching people, specifically on mindset and career transformation."

There's nothing like events beyond a man's control and ability to manage to make him pay attention, is there? Why do we wait for the explosions to go off? Why don't we act sooner? In Anil's case, his career was working too well. Why ruin a good thing? As he began coaching others, Anil understood a greater insight from his own wake-up call: The career isn't the problem; we are.

"Everyone I speak to says, 'Oh, my career!' But the deeper you go, the more you find that it's almost never the career. It's everything else that's happening in people's lives, and how it affects their career, that drives them. The COVID-19 pandemic was a good example. I've talked to a lot of people who said they aren't sure they want to go back to what they did before. It's not the job itself; it's how they've changed internally that causes the shift."

Paul's first skirmish with success drove his pride to new, impossible heights. He resigned from a position at a company that had promoted him four times in seven months during a bright moment of an otherwise dark career season.

"I was in customer service and I wanted to make more money by being in sales," he said. "So, I applied, but they dilly-dallied on my transfer. In the meantime, I started thinking some pretty arrogant things, like 'If only they knew how good I am, they'd have transferred me the day I applied.'"

Whoa. Those are dangerous thoughts. Could you be honest and admit to thinking like that? Or maybe you don't talk that way about yourself, but you're very good at criticizing or backstabbing others. "I was terribly envious of people," Paul added. "Scorn, contempt, sarcasm—you name it, I harbored it. I wondered how people could possibly be content to just 'work a job.' I wanted to change the world, and I thought myself very important. But nothing I did career-wise measured up, so I was also sullen and depressed." He wrestled those demons for two decades.

Curtis's career became multidimensional during his time with Dow, even though it got derailed by forced retirement. "What we call 'our job' isn't actually OUR job," he said. "It's important to remember that the position belongs to the company, not to you."

Curtis' story pained me when I heard it. He had a successful corporate career of thirty years with a great salary, benefits and multiple levels of promotion. He is a "people builder" by nature and became a career counselor and consultant within the Dow footprint. If anyone qualified for the gold watch/pension/caretaker retirement from a company that could afford to do it. Curtis did. But none of that mattered when they pulled the plug on him.

Scott's trajectory changed when his wife of twenty-three years, Ashley, taught him to view his life through the paradigm of process. The Beebes (pronounced bee-bees) track and quantify literally every detail of life they can. "We have a slogan, 'Spreadsheets Change Lives!'" said Scott. "A date night is an event on a calendar, and a calendar is a spreadsheet. If we can leverage tools like spreadsheets to allocate time, money and resources, we can track progress. When we can measure progress, we can then filter it through the lenses of humanity, heart, and soul."

Seth had a chip on his shoulder, growing up in a commune in the woods. "The people there didn't value education, and I felt like a second-class citizen. I wanted to prove everyone wrong, so I thought to myself, 'I'll do it a different way.'"

And off Seth went; He married his high school sweetheart and went into business with his father. Over time, he found success. They eventually sold the business they'd started for millions of dollars, propelling Seth into a long career in consulting, financing and owning businesses. But he felt "disappointed—like a failure, even with a lot of success."

That's got to be rough. You get the girl, make a fortune, and prove everyone wrong, but you're still unhappy.

What does it look like to thrive in career?

Anil said we should carefully distinguish between "career change" and "career transformation." The way he described it, only one of them really goes with thriving.

"People come to me and say, 'I want a career change.' They're after a superficial change, such as job title or employer. But once you start digging in and understanding someone as a person, you find out why they really want to change." It's not the job or the rank, in other words. We're tired of ourselves, as we currently are.

Anil's own transformation revealed this. "I wanted to make the switch to become an entrepreneur and help people," he said, "but it didn't start by changing my title. I found myself working on spirituality and my health, of all things. Switching job titles or changing ownership doesn't alter character. That's why we go beneath the surface when people complain about their careers."

Paul grew to distrust isolation so much that he describes his daily life as "Never truly alone. Physically, I'm alone," he said. "I'm by myself in my home. But spiritually, I'm escorted everywhere by 'bodyguards' whose main job is to protect me from myself. If I make poor decisions in isolation, the solution is to run them through my 'handlers,' the way the President of the United States has 'handlers.'" There's a good example of someone who never makes decisions alone!

"Whenever there's growth, success, development, or maturity in my life, I'm surrounded by the right people," Paul continued. "I have a great group of peers and external leadership counsel. And when there's failure, disappointment, and things go downhill, it's because I make decisions in isolation."

Paul's last insurance job fired him a few years ago. In response, he began his entrepreneurial journey. He now leads a team of young writers and creatives at his ghost-writing agency, The Reluctant Thought Leader.

Curtis' long season in the corporate world, and his present-day influence as the founder of MyCareerQuest, showcase what's possible, even when you do everything right and the bottom still drops out. During his time at Dow, Curtis acquired a unique skill set he could leverage later in life. That's important to remember. If you're currently doing work that doesn't align with your core, you'll still pick up useful skills and knowledge along the way.

Curtis realized losing his role was not, in fact, the "beginning of the end," but rather, as Churchill might say, "the end of the beginning." Leaving Dow sparked a period of grief as he adjusted to the loss of a very strong platform he'd built over decades.

"I struggled to find my voice for some time after that," he said. "But when the smoke cleared, I latched onto something I'd been doing pro bono for Dow—career counseling. Of course, the people who need career counseling the most—young people—can't afford it. But we had done it for my own daughter, so I figured there had to be a way to pursue it and earn an income from it." Long after Dow terminated Curtis' position, there's still plenty of work to do to influence next generations.

You can imagine the detailed spreadsheets and analytics governing Scott's thriving life and business. "We have one called a 'Culture Calendar,'" he said. "It lines out week by week, year by year. The vertical axis represents raising the bar in your culture—in weekly team meetings, project meetings, remembering birthdays and so forth."

Whether you're growing a business or not, you create culture—in your home, church, community association, and workplace. Scott used the example of how whiskey is distilled to point out how cultures are shaped. The more times one distills whiskey, the more they extract the right kind of ingredients. When combined, these ingredients make it a popular beverage. So, how does this apply to the culture you're building or the career you're pursuing?

Well, it goes right back to the concept we discussed in relationships—growth versus decay. If you're constantly "distilling" yourself through practices like accountability, transparency, and oversight from a caring group of peers, you'll enter your career and workplace with an exceptional cultural influence. If you own a business, and you're constantly teaching, communicating and reviewing everything you do, you'll eventually attract the right people into the right seats. And that's what takes you from "good" to "great," as Jim Collins famously wrote. "On the other hand, if the ingredients are destructive, such as greed, subversion, or gossip, don't be surprised when people walk out in handcuffs," Scott warned.

Seth similarly connected career thriving with a growth-versus-fixed mindset and gratitude for what we currently have. "What are you doing to reach your potential?" he asked. "If you can answer [that question], you're growing and thriving. I often ask myself whether things I care about meet 'tests' in my life. One of them is steward-ship because we don't define our potential for ourselves. God does that."

Okay, fine. But what if you don't know your "potential"? What if you haven't discovered it yet? Seth answered, "It's unlikely you'll be an expert in multiple fields. You may need a new job or a new company in the same field you're in now. If you find one, and you still don't thrive there, then you might want to shift fields. But remember all the expertise you've gathered and the connections you've made when you do."

Is thriving in career worth it?

If you develop the kind of self-awareness these men have, you may start to notice patterns—recurring elements that crop up for you. Many of us in the world of coaching, for example, give off a magnetic "pull" for people who want advice. Even if my day job involved bricklaying, people would still approach me to ask for guidance. It's something I radiate subconsciously.

No, this doesn't mean you can quit your job just yet. But if you accept the intentionality of the world we live in, is it possible that these things happen because it's your destiny? What if you're already being called? What should you do in the meantime? There's no need to interpret your current situation as punishment, abandonment, or betrayal. As you've already heard, there are things to be grateful for in the present moment just as it is.

But if your career feels like a wet blanket, could you look deeper? Would you be willing to get beneath your own surface with caring, trusted outside eyes to help? Wouldn't you want to uncover what's really bugging you and pursue a renewed and updated version of yourself?

Could you stay where you are and learn to be faithful with small things until the day God promotes you? I don't write this lightly; I know something of the despair, monotony, and dysfunction you deal with. But could you trust God and let the hardship complete its lesson?

Is it possible that some habits these men developed—prayer, journaling, reflection, meditation, and solitude with God—could help sustain you through this time? Maybe you don't need a new job, but your job needs a new you. This goes for your current position and any new ones.

You'll find alignment more directly when you involve outside eyes—your spouse, perhaps, or a mentor. Your mind will begin to look for whatever you write on paper as you go about your day. And when people in authority come into contact with your degree of clarity, it'll be clear—either they'll be a pathway to your potential or an obstacle.

If you choose the path of learning from your plight, you can't lose. No one harms their own life by doing the right thing and owning their circumstances with honor. Either you'll find peace and balance in your current career/occupation and grow there, or you'll eventually transition into your true calling. But this only happens after you do the deep, dirty work first.

You can find additional resources for career by listening to the Made to Thrive *podcast episodes featuring these men, or by visiting amithriving.com*

Chapter Eight:

THE ANSWER
TO THE QUESTION

"And for us this is the end of all the stories, and
we can most truly say that they all lived happily
ever after. But for them it was only the beginning
of the real story. All their life in this world and all
their adventures in Narnia had only been the cover
and the title page: now at last they were beginning
Chapter One of the Great Story which no one on
earth has read: which goes on for ever: in which
every chapter is better than the one before."
— **C.S. Lewis,** *The Last Battle*

f you're reading this chapter, your journey through this book has taken one of three courses—unless you're like my wife and just skipped to the end to see how everything turned out:

1. You read the book in its entirety.
2. You read the introduction, took the assessment, and read the chapter(s) about the areas of your life that need the most attention.
3. You read the introduction, took the assessment, and jumped to the conclusion.

As I said in the introduction, I designed this book to help you, so I'm good with whichever road you took to get here. But let's quickly recap, so we're all on the same page:

In the introduction, I shared my moment of realizing that I wasn't thriving and that I didn't know how to. I hypothesized twelve reasons why I (and maybe you and certainly most men we know) wasn't living fully in the 7 Core Areas: Faith, identity, mission, career, health, relationships, and finances.

With my hypotheses in hand, I used the scientific method, albeit anecdotally, gathering data in thirty-nine interviews with men who thrive in at least one area. I asked each person these 5 Big Questions:

1. Why aren't more men thriving? What's holding them back?
2. When weren't you thriving? What changed?

3. What does it look like to thrive?
4. What tools, resources, strategies do you recommend?
5. What encouragement do you have for men who want to thrive? (Is thriving in this area worth it?)

The results identified three important themes, regardless of the Core Area we discussed.

THE THREE REASONS YOU AREN'T THRIVING

I really didn't know what I would discover, and the findings amazed me. In almost every interview—no matter which Core Area or amount of life experience—three themes emerged that pointed to the answer of why men don't thrive:

1. A lack of vision
2. A lack of community
3. A lack of knowledge

Time and again, one, two or all three of these deficits provided the reason the contributors to the book either weren't thriving in the past or how they began to thrive when they added that piece of the puzzle to their lives. Let's look at each of these individually.

1. A Lack of Vision

Your first inclination (depending on your familiarity with the Bible) might be to think of Proverbs 29:18 here—

people perish when they don't have a vision The vision missing from many men's lives comes in three parts:

First, there is the obvious idea of vision as seeing what can be. This future pacing of your life is popular in many goal setting programs (including mine!). I love its ability to create positive tension in our lives, measured by the distance between where we are and where we'd like to be.

When men lack this type of vision, it can lead to a lack of motivation in daily life and what I experienced in my early thirties: An uninspiring and disappointing prediction of what the next four decades would be like. I recall a friend of mine who had reached a similar point in life. He had a good job, a nice house, an engaging social life, but no vision of life being any better or more exciting. Sitting by the pool one summer afternoon, he asked himself, "Should I start smoking pot?" Pick your poison, but a lack of a compelling vision, one that literally forces you to move toward it, is a big contributor to the distractions we actively seek out and eventually consume us.

Second, a lack of vision in a man's life can also mean not seeing what is right in front of us. John Eldredge's *Wild at Heart* identifies three main core desires of a man's life: A battle to fight, an adventure to live, a beauty to rescue. Absent these, we resign ourselves to a boring existence, one we escape with video games, movies, sports (fantasy, rec, and spectator), and/or porn. But clear vision helps a man see what is, what exists here and now.

We have a battle to fight (our mission), an adventure to live (our legacy), and a beauty to rescue (our wives), but we just don't see it. We have become accustomed—numb even—to our surroundings and to the needs of those around us. People need us to see them. And once we have that vision, we have a reason to thrive.

The third meaning of vision is example. Men don't thrive because they lack real-life examples of what it looks like to thrive. You may recall my interview with health coach Kevin Davis in Chapter Five. He helps people live with more energy, so they can do the things they want to do for years and even decades. I asked him, "How do I know that there's a higher level of health to operate at?" In other words, how do I know I'm not already thriving?

His answer reveals the third problem of vision: "If you see someone your age doing something you can't, there's room for improvement." Unfortunately, we often don't have enough people in our lives who thrive in more than one or two of the Core Areas. The fact that you're reading this book might mean that you're the most fully alive of the people around you! Who are you supposed to be learning from? Who is giving you a tangible vision of how to live? When men lack an example of thriving, they tend to settle for less than what God wants for them.

2. A Lack of Community

The next big reason why men don't thrive—and a common impetus for the change that so many interviewees made in their lives—is community, which I'll also call brotherhood. This includes and extends our discussion of vision because community also provides examples to model. Beyond this, community serves two vital roles in a man's quest to thrive:

First, community keeps us from isolation. I'm not talking about being a hermit or living only online. No, the worst isolation actually appears to be socially engaged. On the surface, many men go to church, connect with colleagues in the office and after work, participate in their kids' activities and go on dates with their wives. But almost all of those interactions are superficial. There are very few people who truly know this man. And there are few things more dangerous than a man who's alone.

When we find ourselves isolated from other men, we don't see the impact of our behavior— the effect of what we do with our lives. When we lack true brothers, we lack insight into what's really going on internally, often until it's too late. Then, we have an affair, get addicted to something, or lose credibility with our kids. Once those things happen, an isolated man has an even tougher road home.

The second benefit of brotherhood—and one that's a bit more hopeful—is a group of fellow travelers. Road trips are just more fun when you bring some friends along, and the band of brothers we journey with not only help us thrive, but make life more enjoyable. Finding your brotherhood taps into Jim Rohn's rule of five: You become most like the five people you spend the most time with. And if you're becoming more and more like them, then your wife and children are vicariously interacting with them more and more. Choose men who make you better just by being around them.

When intentionally deciding who you interact with on a regular basis—be it in person or online—you're voting for the life you want to have. Your brotherhood may change actors from time to time as some men walk with you just for a season, but it can be key to why you're not thriving—and how you can.

3. A Lack of Knowledge

The third—and the most simple—reason I heard over and over again as I interviewed more than three dozen men about why men aren't thriving? We struggle with a lack of knowledge. In a world of immediate access to seemingly infinite information, how can we lack knowledge? Easy: We choose to.

Most of us have a level of competence in a few of the Core Areas; however, our tendency is to stick with what we're good at and avoid what we're not. For example, you might have a superb and meaningful career and live a healthy lifestyle, but your checkbook (remember those?) and your relationship with your son aren't so great.

In this situation, are you more likely to have a real conversation with your wife about your finances or spend some time on a project at work that has your interest? Are you more likely to push through the awkward one-word answers your child gives you after school—so you can find out how his day really was—or hit the gym on the way home from the office? If you're anything like me, feeling incompetent isn't something I gravitate toward. I tend to double down on what I'm naturally good at.

There are two problems with that strategy (if you can call a default a strategy): First, our lives are really out of balance! Each of the 7 Core Areas is essential. Pretending that some of them don't exist robs us of the rich experience God calls us to and can sometimes hinder the areas where we're experiencing success.

Second, when we wake up to the fact that we need to improve in a particular area, we don't have time to fiddle around with various solutions. We need to know what works, and we need to put it into practice quickly. Our atrophied skills in some areas won't sustain the momentum we need to make substantive change. We need to rely on what others have experienced and taught so we can employ their wisdom, knowing what to do and when. We are destroyed by our lack of knowledge. So, now what?

Conclusion:

WHAT DO I DO NOW?

We've owned that we aren't thriving, at least not in all 7 Core Areas. We've discovered three core reasons for this disconnect between the lives God has called us to and the lives we currently live. So, now what?

First, create your vision. In Habakkuk 2:2, God tells Habakkuk to "write the vision; make it plain on tablets, so he may run who reads it." Your vision for the future should excite you because God gives it to you. He gives us the desires of our heart, so spend time thinking about what you desire for the future!

Second, become very intentional about your brother-hood. Simply begin by taking stock of whom you spend the most time with and who your mentors are. Don't be judg-mental, but ask yourself: Are these the type of men you'd like to become? Are they doing better than you in some of the 7 Core Areas? Do you want your children to become like them?

If you don't have brothers in your life—men who are also intent on thriving and are excited about journeying with you—I invite you to join the Made to Thrive Broth-erhood. This is a community of men who will encourage you, celebrate with you, and sometimes kick your butt, so you can become a better version of yourself. Check out whyarentmenthriving.com/brotherhood.

Third, begin your Virtuous Cycle. It's not enough to thrive in just one or two of the 7 Core Areas. We're called to much more than that, not just for ourselves—although the rewards are incredible—but for those we're called to impact. While most of us have heard of a 'vicious cycle' (unfortunately by experience), a virtuous cycle takes us up rather than down. What makes the virtuous cycle more dif-ficult, however, is that we're fighting gravity. It's easier to go down than up. However, once you create the momentum required, you can set yourself up for a continuous state of improvement with far less effort.

The Virtuous Cycle is a system of personal growth and self-improvement, both sustainable and applicable across all areas of your life. We use this system each month in the

Brotherhood to get better, one day at a time. We use techniques, strategies, and tools to learn more, apply quickly and scaffold our wins regularly. If you'd like to learn more about The Virtuous Cycle system, visit WhyArentMen-Thriving.com/cycle.

LET'S THRIVE TOGETHER.

I set out to discover why men aren't thriving, which I've spent the majority of this chapter detailing. I hope you've seen some of yourself in my findings, but not to make you feel bad. Instead, think of it like a visit to the doctor (you know, like you did ten years ago. You really should go again soon. And so should I). At the doctor's office, an accurate diagnosis leads to an effective treatment plan.

My second conclusion, however, is probably more exciting: There are so many men who are thriving out there! Until I started looking for them, I didn't realize it. It astonished me how many men kick butt in at least some of the Core Areas. It inspired me to learn from them. This is exciting because they really aren't that different from you and me. Each of them had—and continue to have—times when they weren't thriving. Each of them took steps to start thriving. Now, they share their journey with others, leading with their podcasts, books, courses, and their lives.

And so can you.

Honestly, I actually teared up a bit when I wrote that sentence (and my wife will tell you that's a rarity), because I know you are so close to a life worth living—a life that is an example to your kids, one that legacies are built on. If "the glory of God is a man fully alive," your full, abundant, thriving life—the one you may not have ever known was possible or the one you put up on a shelf long ago—will release God's glory.

"In the same way, let your light shine before others, so that they may see your good works and give glory to your Father who is in heaven" (Matthew 5:16).

We were made to thrive.

Let's get moving. Together.

ABOUT THE AUTHOR

Sam Feeney is an author (obviously!), speaker, and strategist who is passionate about helping men live more effectively, so they can create a bigger impact on their families, communities, and the world. He started Made to Thrive as a resource for men who want to be encouraged, equipped, and empowered to take on whatever God has prepared for them.

After twenty years as a teacher and school counselor, Sam and his family moved from Pennsylvania to Colorado and started their lives anew in an act of faith. This dramatic change marked the beginning of Made to Thrive and Sam's new career in the online space, where he has found a greater reach for his podcast and resources, including this book. When he's not spreading the message of *Why Aren't You Thriving?* as a guest on podcasts, he loves speaking to mission-driven companies and men's groups.

You can learn more about Sam's latest projects and get in touch with him at samfeeney.com or madetothrive. coach/contact.

A free ebook edition is available with the purchase of this book.

To claim your free ebook edition:

1. Visit MorganJamesBOGO.com
2. Sign your name CLEARLY in the space
3. Complete the form and submit a photo of the entire copyright page
4. You or your friend can download the ebook to your preferred device

Print & Digital Together Forever.

Snap a photo

Free ebook

Read anywhere

9 781631 959417